D1612450

DAVID W. HILL

MORAL GRAVITY

Staying Together at the End of the World

BRISTOL
UNIVERSITY
PRESS

First published in Great Britain in 2022 by

Bristol University Press
University of Bristol
1–9 Old Park Hill
Bristol
BS2 8BB
UK
t: +44 (0)117 374 6645
e: bup-info@bristol.ac.uk

Details of international sales and distribution partners are available at
bristoluniversitypress.co.uk

British Library Cataloguing in Publication Data
A catalogue record for this book is available from the British Library

ISBN 978-1-5292-2266-1 hardcover
ISBN 978-1-5292-2267-8 ePub
ISBN 978-1-5292-2268-5 ePdf

Cover design: blu inc
Front cover image: iStock/JacquesPALUT
Bristol University Press uses environmentally responsible
print partners.
Printed in CPI Group (UK) Ltd, Croydon, CR0 4YY

For Mick Hill, my dad.

Contents

Notes on the Author

David W. Hill is Senior Lecturer in Sociology at York St John University. He works as a social theorist specializing in 20th-century French thought, with a particular focus on the work of Emmanuel Levinas, Jean-François Lyotard and Paul Virilio. His research centres on questions of moral experience as they relate to environmental issues, digital technologies and logistical worlds. David is the author of *The Pathology of Communicative Capitalism* (2015).

Before

It is tempting to imagine that we are at present before the catastrophe. Extreme weather and record temperatures and rapid flooding and forest fires would then all be precursors to a disaster that belongs to the future.

We know now that climate change will likely move through threshold transitions rather than in a steady train of accumulative destruction, lurching suddenly and unstoppably into conditions that we cannot turn back. But this is not the same as imagining that environmental catastrophe itself lies ahead of us. The raging storms and burning bushes and creeping deserts and silent extinctions are not precursors but mereological parts of an extant catastrophe that will merely continue to devour whole worlds of life. It has already arrived and is still to come.

To be before catastrophe is to imagine that the catastrophe is an interruptive event, with its own temporal dimensions, that somehow derails the normal course of happenings, that hurls us into a now radically alien lifeworld. Such an event has the extraordinary impact familiar to our disaster imaginary: the biblical flood or the asteroid strike or the worldwide contagion that wipes us all out in hasty devastation. We imagine some deleterious happening befalls us and then in turn we might imagine that there is a possible future marked by our falling, a cliff-edge point where suddenly the familiar ground disappears from beneath our feet, and we fall into despair and into oblivion.

But environmental catastrophe is not one possible future; it is the production of the present. The Anthropocene is marked by human activity having become the most salient factor shaping the geological record. When it is said to have begun makes a difference, since each starting point suggests a different critical emphasis: the Columbian Exchange and the injustices of colonialism; the Industrial Revolution and the exploitations of capital; the Great Acceleration and the risks of technological advance (see Yusoff, 2018a). But when we talk of an Anthropocene, we are already talking about colonialism and capitalism and technoscientific development. We are already forced to confront human cruelty. We are already in the world that our own hubris has imagined.

This is the vantage point of the present book. Not to look backwards at where it all began and how we came to be here, as vital as this is, but to look forwards from here, to imagine what it would take to look forwards and see more than nothing. Jeremy Davies (2016: 40) argues that 'global warming is not an imminent threat but the new condition of the earth'. We cannot afford to look to the future and fear what we might lose of the present; the past conditions of the earth, that have for thousands of years provided a stable and temperate climate, that have made possible the human societies recorded in our histories and our culture, are receding from our grasp. The present is a fiction, an artificial point plotted somewhere amid the whirling confluence of the past and the future. We imagine ourselves treading water as we are dragged out to sea. We imagine ourselves heirs of societies we can no longer have. The world we knew is not in crisis, which, as Bonneuil and Fressoz (2017: 21) point out, suggests a transitory state that might be rolled back. We cannot go back.

Not all of us have been masquerading in the present. Who is the *Anthropos* of the Anthropocene? 'As the Anthropocene proclaims the language of species life', writes Kathryn Yusoff (2018a: 2), 'it really erases the histories of racism that were incubated through the regulating structure of geologic relations'. All periodization comes with the threat of totality. The Anthropocene, as a geological category, must not occlude imperialist projects of anti-blackness that both contribute to the destruction of the world and concentrate that destruction in the lifeworld of the victims of colonialism. The extraction and exploitation of the things of the world, and those reduced to the status of things in this world, imperils us all, but our lives are differently precarious, and our catastrophe unfolds in empirically divergent fashion. Those who have found such profit in extraction and exploitation will hold out the longest; its victims will be hit first and hit worst.

Environmental catastrophe thrives in the gap between the universal and the particular. We masquerade in the present when we acknowledge climate change but not its local manifestations. There is no solution that can keep in place inequality. There is no way forward that allows us to bring with us our hatred of our neighbours or the parochialism of our ethics or the chauvinism of our moral categories. There is no resistance to something that threatens to destroy all life that allows already for lives to be destroyed. The Anthropocene does not universalize our condition, but it must force us out from our imperialism – an imperialism of the same, the tyranny of the hypostatic present, of my self-regard at the top of the hierarchy of suffering – and lead us out towards other lives.

As Bignall and Braidotti (2019: 4) argue, we require local and perspectival solutions to a problem that threatens all life, human and non-human, and not just the imposition of the schemes of the West and the wealthy. The history of capitalism is a history of the exploitation of cheap nature and the burning of fossil fuels (see Moore, 2015; Angus, 2016; Malm, 2016). Increasingly we turn to the corporate executive and the entrepreneur for hope, and yet these personifications of capital are in this elevated position, with its illusion of authority and responsibility, because of their prioritization of capital. As Ian Angus (2016: 114) observes, they are unlikely, in the final reckoning, to put the future of life on earth ahead of an ideology of endless economic growth. Mann and Wainwright (2018) argue that there is no market solution to a problem bound up with the logic of the market; however sincere our saviours might be, they belong to a class of people who are constitutionally incapable of seeing environmental catastrophe as anything but a market failure with a market solution – and so are ultimately incapable of seeing the catastrophe at all. Wright and Nyberg (2015: 3) note this pharmacological function of the corporation, simultaneously responsible for the lion's share of carbon emissions in the global economy and yet held up as our best chance of reducing those emissions through technological innovation. But our tech entrepreneurs only appear to be selling us the hope of geoengineering our climate or the dream of escaping to other planets; these are merely carpet samples for the hegemony of neoliberal capitalism – their solutions serve the interests and identities of the dominant.

If we are to talk of an Anthropocene, then we must avoid the disfigurements of the world that brought us here: that the human is at the centre of all things; that capitalist development is social progress; that the world was not already ending where we did not care to look. And if we are to talk of an Anthropocene then we must at the same time, and as Donna Haraway (2016: 100) implores, talk of making it as short as possible. Ingrid Parker (2017) argues that coming to terms with the Anthropocene – curtailing it, even – is made difficult by our ecological amnesia and by our ecological blindness: we do not remember so well ecology past; and the changes that take us away from that past happen at speeds and at levels we rarely perceive. We need, then, a more expansive openness to the world, an uprightness in the world that is not borne of human chauvinism but of the need to be attentive to everyone and everything – and that aims at the upbuilding of this world together.

Because we are not falling. The world was not firmly beneath our feet, and it will not be suddenly taken out from under us. The future is made by our relationships with others. It is consummated in the encounter with humans and animals and plants; in the encounter with the lithic and the elemental; in the encounter with transcendence. Environmental catastrophe is already produced by a relationship with the world that is all present and no future. The choice is to encounter this world of others with an unlimited moral seriousness or else to come face to face with its destruction. The world is changed when we move towards alterity with humility and enthusiasm. It jolts the hypostasis of the individual present and opens on to a future shared. Our devastation comes not from a fall into oblivion but when we reject the gravity of the other.

This book is not a roadmap to recovery; it offers no programme for survival. The practical matter of how we continue to live together must come from listening to those whose existence has been made precarious, those whose suffering has so far been tolerated to bring us to this catastrophe. The work collected here is motivated instead by the idea that what we need is a radicalization of responsibility that is not in itself sufficient, but necessary if we are to listen to a world of others and consummate our future together. In her analysis of geoengineered solutions to climate change, Holly Buck (2019: 244) argues that we are missing some account of moral accountability, but this seems to be posed in terms of a kind of moral bureaucracy, and it runs counter to María Puig de la Bellacasa's (2017) call to leave behind moral systems and emphasize care as mending and maintenance. Our radicalization of morality is pitched somewhere between these positions. Let responsibility be the harsh name for the pull of the other, the demand for care and for love and for response. And then life would be accountable to life *qua* living.

Bonneuil and Fressoz (2017: xiii) call for 'a revolution in morality and thought' to address the human impact on the world. Such an undertaking would contribute to Félix Guattari's (2018) ecosophical revolution of the political and the social and the cultural, the radical reshaping of the material and immaterial production and reproduction of human existence. At the heart of this is a demand for resingularization:

There is at least a risk that there will be no more human history unless humanity undertakes a radical reconsideration of itself. We must ward off, by every means possible, the entropic rise of a dominant subjectivity. Rather than remaining subject, in perpetuity, to the seductive efficiency of economic competition, we must reappropriate universes of value so that processes of singularization can rediscover their consisting. We need new social and aesthetic practices, new practices of the Self in relation to the other, to the foreign, the strange. (Guattari, 2018: 46–7)

The spirit of this resingularization might be found in Judith Butler's (2016) argument that all life is animated and bound together by its vulnerability, by the interdependence of precarious life and precarious life, by the demand not only to preserve that life but to make all life more liveable; in Haraway's (2016) call to stay with the trouble, forming new kinships, human and non-human, to find ways of living together and living together well; in Deborah Rose's (2017) account of extinction as an unravelling, the sadness of interdependence becoming a peril, one world disappearing and then another in its wake, until whole universes of shared lives diminish, and in her argument that human exceptionalism must end, that the human must be placed where it belongs, in these now unravelling meshes of varied life; and in Anna Tsing's (2017) observation that, when life on earth is so precarious, we should rage against those who put us in this position, of course, but also look to the world, find its strangeness, and attempt to embrace it, however much it challenges the imagination.

Underpinning these approaches would need to be an account of responsibility based on humility and enthusiasm to combat the hubris and the cruelty that have brought us all here. The account that emerges through each of the chapters of this book is as follows:

The world is not a stage on which we act. It is not a surface for the conduct of human activity. We do not go into the world – we are of it. This is a world of varied and precarious existences. But what is precarious to a degree is always already vulnerable to me. Ours is a world of encounters. To encounter is to negotiate the existence of these others. This is not a negotiation of terms but an adaptation of my existence to the presence of the other existence. To live with others is to live otherwise than our own adventures. That we might exist without concern for how our existence might engulf the other is the origin of their precarity. It takes humility to recognise this, that there is this other existence, that its existence is endangered by my egoism, that its place in this world is not mine to grasp. The other would then exceed me. Here there must be humility, a sense that there are existences that I cannot fathom, ways of being in the world that are threatened if I act with obliviousness or vanity. And then there would be an enthusiasm for this existence and for its preservation and for its elevation in the world. I would make my self-regard small and my embrace large to better encounter the wonderful magnitude of the world and its beings and its things, even if in holding these others dear they ultimately elude me. Humility comes from the encounter with the graveness of the other existence, the moral seriousness of its vulnerability to me. Enthusiasm is to accede to the pull of the other, the moral demand that emanates not from me but that orients me in my response and draws me away from myself. We can act without humility and without enthusiasm but neither inaction removes this moral gravity. To act without regard for the other is to inflate the present with the egoism of a solitary existence. To live in response to the other is to break free from the confines of this withdrawn now and to embrace a future marked most profoundly by alterity. We exist responsibly or we have no future.

This way of understanding a responsibility that is of the world is motivated in large part by the work of Emmanuel Levinas. In texts like *Totality and Infinity* (2007) and *Otherwise than Being* (2008b) Levinas gives us an account of morality, not as a calculation of how to live well, but as existence itself. It is furnished with an understanding of responsibility that is radical insofar as it rejects the accountancy of blame and the bureaucracy of permissible actions. It is radical to the extent that it prioritizes an understanding of responsibility that would exceed all rules or norms or social expectations, because it responds infinitely to the other's need rather than operating within a regulatory framework. And it is radical insomuch as it rejects the totalizing impulse of Western metaphysics and leaves space for an encounter with the transcendent. Levinas gives us, most importantly, a sense of 'the gravity of the other' (2008b: 118). But he could be more radical. Levinas's other is a human other. His responsibility is not open to the animal or the plant, to the stone or the sea, the light or the wind. As we will see, this way of thinking morally can give urgency to our hopelessness and give cause to resist the draw of those who tell us our future lies away from this earth. But to fully motivate either position we need to embrace more than human encounters. If we are running out of time, then we must be bold in what we take seriously and unembarrassed by what might pull us close.

How do we imagine a future that is consummated in the encounter? And what if we're fucked anyway? A future made in the movement towards an inaccessible other is fundamentally unknowable. But the overconfidence of the present is overcome if we anticipate the very worst, even if we cannot comprehend the ruination of worlds it brings. Such an approach is inspired by the work of Paul Virilio, and in particular the ethos captured in his *Politics of the Very Worst* (1999), an interview (with Philippe Petit) that reveals his commitment to a critical and productive pessimism. Much of the book deals with various technological advances, advancing then Virilio's position that there can be no progress with technology if there is no criticism of technology. Without a certain pessimism about where it will take us, there is only conditioning by technology, and the obscuring of its myriad pollutions (environmental and experiential) and the accidents it harbours. Let the advertisers be optimistic, he says; let those who consider the politics of these technologies anticipate the very worst. 'I am not a prophet of doom', says Virilio (1999: 13), 'but simply a true lover of the new technologies'.

Despite providing the title of the book, a politics of the very worst is not systematically cashed out in its pages. Reading between the lines, and extending beyond the narrower focus on technology, a politics of the very worst is already in place as the colonization of the lifeworld by an organization of the world that creates catastrophe, and it would be opposed by an ethics of the very worst, which would seek to revalue and reanimate life as experience, experience of a world shared with others, to go beyond this catastrophe. Political battles about how we live in sustainable lifeworlds have been lost; we must fight now for the vitality of those lifeworlds against their immiseration by the politics of progress and accumulation. This is our moral revolution: to be true lovers of all others and defenders of their infinite worlds.

Something firmer, more shape giving, can be made of Virilio's approach to the very worst if it is imbued with a sociological imagination. In the classic account of the sociological imagination provided by C. Wright Mills (1967), personal troubles must be connected to social issues. 'Neither the life of an individual nor the history of a society can be understood without understanding both', writes Mills (1967: 3). Without this, we would be rendered 'morally insensible' by social change that outpaces the individual and blurs their orientation of the self in accordance with values, values that Mills says may be threatened by change, but we should add might also themselves threaten us with the deleterious. The backdrop to individual anxieties about climate change is a social indifference to the effects of the human activities that accelerate it. Our future will be decided behind our backs if we cannot situate our hopelessness in hope, and not only our troubles in issues. To situate hopelessness in hope we must confront the very worst and its obliteration of infinite individual worlds so that we might turn to infinity and find there our relationship to the other and to the future of alterity that might nurture us.

A sociology of the very worst – an elaboration of Virilio's looser ethics of the very same – would use the cataclysmic to explore the location of the individual within a world of others and to put in relief the experience of sociality and the formation of social relationships. It is organized on the principle that not only does an anticipation of the very worst reveal something of the nature of subjects and institutions and organizations, but also that the sociality and moral constitution of the subject is formed by this anticipation. It is undertaken in a mode of critical pessimism that would anticipate the worst to reveal objects of criticism before they reach the point of negation. All pessimism is like this to the extent that it imagines a future that is only inescapable insofar as the change needed to avoid it is presently unimaginable. To anticipate the very worst is to at least grasp the magnitude of quite how radical the alternative is. We give up hope only to find it in our urgent responsibility for others. We see our interdependence in this image of oblivion that makes our egoism and our inattention and our refusal of the other appear in their fullest weakness. And by doing so we prepare the ground to recognize those local and perspectival solutions to global cataclysm. This sociology of the very worst motivates a revolution in morality that makes possible an environmentalism of precarious lives.

This book is comprised of four chapters – interrupted by an excursion on humanism and halted by a tentative if concluding statement – that combine to make a case for the desirability of this manner of thinking about environmental catastrophe.

Pessimism asks what it might mean to approach all this with the acceptance that 'we're fucked', that we have fucked it, that we are already dead. Such an acceptance need not be a nihilism nor a narcissistic melancholy. We could make of it instead a recognition of a collective death, that all death is the death of another, and that the death of the other is the very worst thing that can happen to me and so binds me in a community of infinite moral relations. We could see in it the urgency of finding cause together, recognizing that no individual can speak for a future that is consummated with others, that instead we face its radical contingency in radical activity together that breaks with the eternal same of our present stasis. And we can embolden that activity with the recognition that any contemplation of the enormity of our task together demands humility and enthusiasm, the very stuff of a revolutionary responsibility oriented in the other's regard. As a statement, 'we're fucked' would then pick out not our giving up but a confrontation with the moral gravity of our existence.

Exodus then suggests that if we are to have all this then it must be here. We find hope in hopelessness and not in the false hopes of quick-fix solutions that follow the same line of flight that brought us to catastrophe. Should we escape our stricken planet and live on Mars? When we leave the earth's gravity we lose the depth of our experience here with others, swapping encroaching desertification for the desert of space. These visions of off-world salvation demand the reduction of human diversity to a mass of cargo to be torn from relation with a world of others and deposited on distant planets or moons or asteroids. This is entirely in line with the operation of those who advance such solutions, the tech entrepreneurs who want to continue the rapacious colonization of the world and its immiseration of the life-size, only now in space, and who approach our environmental catastrophe as a risk management exercise, and so do not confront it at all. We stay together here because to go elsewhere is already our undoing.

At this point there is an *Interruption* in the form of a brief meditation on Levinas's humanism, his humanism, that is, of the other, the way that it embraces the interruption of the self by what lies outside it, and on the necessity of interrupting the narrowness of its embrace of the human only, without losing the humanness of its vantage point. We are then not interrupted by catastrophe but by the other; our catastrophe is the refusal of this interruption by everyone and by everything.

Responsibility then set outs the case for a togetherness that includes non-human animals. Such an account does not demand that the animal is responsible in my direction, although it cannot be ruled out. More vitally, the moral seriousness of the animal cannot be denied in advance of the encounter because it is here, in confrontation with vulnerability, that our humility and our enthusiasm are evoked, that the other animal would exceed the human whose responsibility is then given in its direction. This vulnerability is only encountered if we demand of ourselves the urgent task of listening to animals who do not speak our language but who communicate the precariousness of their existence. We are then bound together with animals that we cannot leave behind nor take into our possession.

Accession finally extends this to non-human non-animal others through an account of being with geology that strives also to bring along with it plant life and the elements as a beginning to a more expansive moral ecology. If the Anthropocene means that the human is now oversized in the geological record, then it is urgent that we take seriously the moral claims of the geological on our existence. Geology both forms and exceeds the human. Our existence is bound up with geological processes and eluded by their deep time and disarming liveliness. Geological entities are not given to the human as a tool or as a surface for its dwelling; they have their own imperative, withdraw from the human approach, and interrupt human endeavour and identity. The encounter with this *geolterity* demands that we give the geological its space, setting aside human notions of persistence and passivity to recognize another precarious existence that draws my responsibility.

These chapters are brought together by an *End* that is not an end, but a recognition that any approach to the end of precarious life posed by environmental catastrophe might be nourished by radicalizations of moral life but that the work it demands remains the work of communities of and with and for the vulnerable. When climate change threatens everything, and there is a need to think otherwise, the work of theory is urgent, but an environmentalism of precarious lives demands the urgent patience that is required of attentiveness to suffering.

This moral gravity is out in the world. And there too is our hope.

ONE

Pessimism

Thought is uncomfortable with catastrophe because it has the sense to recognize the agent of its own undoing. Bernard Stiegler (2018) argues that to look at the reports of the Intergovernmental Panel on Climate Change (IPCC) – of desertification and rising temperatures and warming seas and melting glaciers – is to bring about an expectation of the very worst. The danger is not only that we might choose not to look but that we might refuse the message altogether. The trick, says Stiegler, is to fight against hopeless negativity without denying the legitimacy of this warning. Mann and Wainwright adopt a similar position in their *Climate Leviathan* (2018), that we ought to avoid the conclusion that 'we're fucked' as strenuously we do the idea that technology or the markets or some other utopian intervention might save us.

But there is something ultimately ungenerous about the dismissal of a sentiment like 'we're fucked'. Mann and Wainwright use the expression twice:

Unfortunately, the prospect of rapid environmental change has generally produced an insufficient theoretical response among mainstream 'progressive' thinkers. Most of it is pious utopianism ('ten simple ways to save the planet'), an appeal to market solutions ('cap and trade'), or nihilism ('we're fucked'). These are false solutions. ...

For all its limitations, thoughtful speculation is analytically and politically superior to all the other options currently available: pretending everything is 'normal', embracing the false hopes peddled by techno-utopians, abandoning ourselves to nihilism ('we're fucked'), or, worse still, validating the visions of the apocalyptic books and films that transmute our fears into spectacular, utopian commodities. (2018: xi, 130)

There is, then, on the one hand hope and on the other despair, where both of which are taken to excess. The task of theory, they suggest, is to navigate a path between the two.

Is there a path between the two? Paul Virilio (1986: 47) argues that as the ecological catastrophe deepens, we begin to lose diversity, the world dividing into 'hopeful populations' and 'despairing populations'. Those with hope are those who are allowed to look to the future as one of further accumulation, a possessiveness that grants access to the possible; those with only despair are those that are left to subsist in a finite world they cannot transcend. Virilio is here raising the possibility that hope and despair in the face of catastrophe are not choices or dispositions but classes of experience – or perhaps experiences of classes. Theory has a certain responsibility to the extremity of this experience. The trick is not to avoid the excesses of hope and despair – to locate the most realistic hope and temper it with the least amount of despair possible – but to understand what they communicate and to show what they might achieve. What if 'we're fucked' is not a nihilistic disavowal of the possible but instead a yearning for radical possibility?

For this to be the case, the more pressing danger to avoid is a kind of liberal narcissism. As Kathryn Yusoff (2018a) notes, the Anthropocene portends the end of the world, but worlds have long been ending outside the West, and perhaps what marks the Anthropocene most of all, or at least what gives the concept its impetus, is that certain communities are now noticing this, since it promises to end them too. If the lionized individual of the liberal West is now threatened, then what is needed is something altogether more radical than a kind of liberalism scrambled to emergency stations. As Judith

Butler (2006) argues, lives have long been rendered unliveable by a world view that does not grant full subjectivity to its victims and that codes their deaths as ultimately ungrievable. Nonetheless, Butler sees potential in the foundation of a community based on loss and vulnerability, if we ask: What is left of me when I grieve? What is lost in the other person? The trick, she says, is to avoid narcissistic melancholy and focus on the relational ties of being vulnerable to wounding and to death, of being harmed by the loss of the other, and to include all who lose and are wounded in our concerns. In the context of environmental catastrophe, and between Yusoff and Butler, we can say that if we are to mourn our future loss responsibly, then we need thought that will lead us out towards the suffering already endured.

The task now is to recognize the gravity of the situation in radically moral terms. *We're fucked. We're already dead. As far as I know. But at least there is this 'we'. And so …*

Collective death

'We're fucked' might mean any number of things in the context of climate change, from living under conditions hostile to human life to complete annihilation. In the spirit of the very worst, if we take it to mean something like 'we're dead' – in the sense of 'we've fucked this and we're all going to die' – then it usefully brings together questions of how we cope with an extant and impending catastrophe and how we manage a more general and social experience of death. An understanding of sociality that has finitude at its heart is useful when confronted by an environmental catastrophe that threatens death on a global scale. If we understand that death is something that happens to others but not to the individual, since when death arrives the dead are no longer around, then it might open on to a more communal understanding of the problem we face. The key to this is in recognizing and defending the distinction between a mass death and a collective death, the first passive and anonymous and the second locating an active individual within a moral community.

Nielsen and Skotnicki (2019) argue that finitude – the fact of death as a limit to one's possibilities – is an everyday kind of experience. They draw here on the work of Martin Heidegger in *Being and Time* (2006), and the idea that our lives gain their significance from the limitation of death, such that existence is organized towards finality and that it might be conceived of as a being towards death. According to this view, individuals feel anxious that they cannot escape death and fulfil all their possibilities, and so throw themselves into projects in the present. In such a way, for Heidegger, when we confront our finitude, we can take responsibility for our own lives, recognizing death as 'the possibility of the *im*possibility of existence' (2006: 354, emphasis in original) and using it as a spur to realize our possibilities. Nielsen and Skotnicki use this as the basis for what they call a 'sociology towards death', which gives rise to two very useful organizing concepts: 'existential marginalization', where deprivation leads to a reduced ability to imagine the future; and 'existential exhaustion', where a concern for one's own existence causes stress.

But while Heidegger maintained that no-one could die in my place, there is cause to counter that even the one who dies cannot experience death, that the only experience of death available is the experience of the other's death, viewed from the outside. Maurice Blanchot encapsulates this idea in *The Instant of my Death* (2000), a short story recounting an escaped assassination during the Second World War. Here, a character identified only as 'a young man' (Blanchot, 2000: 3) is accused of resistance activities and put in front of a firing squad. He asks that his family might be spared the sight of his execution, and they go indoors 'as if everything has already been done' (Blanchot, 2000: 5). At this moment, Blanchot (2000: 5, 7) says, the young man is already 'bound to death', has already encountered 'the infinite opening up' and become 'freed from life'. And then there is a commotion, and he gets away. Blanchot tells us that this was nevertheless already the instant of his death, that the young man lives on having already died: 'As if the death outside of him could only henceforth collide with the death in him. "I am alive. No, you are dead"' (Blanchot, 2000: 9). Blanchot concludes: 'All that remains is the feeling of lightness that is death itself or, to put it more precisely, the instant of my death henceforth always in abeyance' (Blanchot, 2000: 11).

Jacques Derrida (2000a) uses this story to explore the tension between fiction and testimony, the changes in perspective revealing that both the young man and the narrator are Blanchot, that Blanchot experienced this event during the war, and that he bears witness to it here as an alibi against bystanding or collaboration. At the same time, Derrida indicates that this story opens onto the phenomenology of death that runs through much of Blanchot's philosophical work. The story is animated by the idea that if no-one can die in my place then no-one can testify to my death but me – and only if I survive it. The only experience of my own death then is its deferral, a death that will come but is presently suspended. And so, the young man escapes the firing squad but not death – as his family seem to acknowledge by their going indoors. As Blanchot (1989: 96) argues, in *The Space of Literature,* 'all the escape routes have to be rejected', death must be accepted as necessary, before we can realize the possibilities of being. This is the sense in which an exterior death collides with an interior death; the anticipation of an imminent death meets finitude as something immanent to existence. The experience of death, then, is only ever an anticipation of death, thinking that you are about to die, thinking that death is to come but it never coming because when it arrives, I have gone. This marks the shift from an 'I' that can announce its existence to the 'you' that marks the end of that existence, the necessity of someone else announcing the death. An 'I' cannot say "I am dead" – only someone else could experience it and so speak of it. This is what Blanchot (1989: 100) calls 'the impossibility of dying'. He says variously that death is necessary, and that death is impossible; it is, as Derrida (2000a: 47) puts it, the 'impossible necessary'. At bottom, for Blanchot (1989: 155), it is not a case of being towards death, as it is for Heidegger, but of death rejecting being even when it produces meaning for existence.

In the face of environmental catastrophe, then, the response 'we're fucked / we're dead' might not be nihilism but instead the anticipation of a death that is necessary but that has not yet made everything impossible. We are already living in a catastrophe that is also still to come. The catastrophe is already our relationship to the world, a way of being that would reject all being. Whether we can avoid fatalism with this depends on whether we see the devastation wrought as a mass death or a collective death. To imagine the very worst that climate change might bring is to imagine sudden and unstoppable extinction. Jeremy Davies (2016) warns that a mass extinction event may be some way off yet, but in terms of geological time we might consider it to be nearly upon us. The problem with orienting ourselves to this is not just temporal, though; the idea of a cataclysmic event that wipes out all of humanity lacks particularity or diversity – in some ways, the thought of the end of humanity lacks humanity before it gets to the end. That is, when we imagine some great extinction event, we imagine a mass and not a collective death. The warning lacks urgency not only because it warns of an event that is far off but also of a death that is generalized.

Blanchot is alive to this in *The Space of Literature*. Here he argues that we want to die on our own terms, to have an individualist death, to be oneself, right up to the end. We do not want to die the anonymous death of *the They* (in the sense of Heidegger's *das Man*): 'Mass-produced death, ready-made in bulk for all and in which each disappears hastily' (Blanchot, 1989: 123). That said, Blanchot warns that while we seek to die a death that does not betray who we are, we can also not escape the way that death exceeds the individual – its transcendence.

We want to say, "I die" and not be a part of a 'they' that died – but we know that an 'I' cannot say its death, that to imagine otherwise is to seek an immortality that is withheld. By extension, in relation to a mass extinction, it might be that we fear an anonymous death but also do not take it seriously enough because it is not the death we have in mind. A mass extinction, much like a biblical flood or an asteroid strike or a supernova explosion, lacks urgency because it is not the death of me, of an individual, but of a crowd. And yet, environmental catastrophe is not an instantaneous or simultaneous death, even though the threshold transitions of climate change might be abrupt (see Clark, 2010). As Rosemary-Claire Collard (2018) points out, extinction is a slow violence, a faltering unravelling, a drawn-out attrition punctuated by dramatic loss.

We should reject the choice of an individualistic death or a mass death and think instead in terms of a collective death. In *The Instant of my Death,* before the commotion that allows the young man to get away, from the firing squad if not from death, Blanchot (2000: 5) writes: 'He was perhaps suddenly invincible. Dead – immortal. Perhaps ecstasy. Rather the feeling of compassion for suffering humanity, the happiness of not being immortal or eternal. Henceforth, he was bound to death by a surreptitious friendship.' Death, Blanchot is telling us, is never purely individual. Death exceeds the individual. Death is not mine, that is, in the way that Heidegger suggests. Derrida (2000a: 69) alights upon this passage only very briefly, highlighting the way that it reveals 'a story of finitude, a friendship with finite beings', or perhaps a 'passion for death' that is manifest as a 'compassion for suffering humanity' and that is then enacted in 'a bond without bond'. This last part (the bond without bond) evokes, without elaboration or naming, but surely deliberately, the moral philosophy of Emmanuel Levinas – and this will be taken up later. For now, we have in mind a death that avoids individualism and the mass and is instead collective insofar as it situates an 'I' with others in a 'we', that same 'we' invoked in the utterance of 'we're fucked /

we're dead'. In anticipating the death that is delayed but never avoided, then, we might participate in a community bound by a shared experience of mortality, where the 'I' is responsible for the others because it recognizes the frailty of their existence and is given its confidence and coherence by responding to this frailty. This would be a community founded on the recognition of the finitude of the other and a compassion for suffering that overflows into a concern for their death. The collective then avoids the mass to the extent that it individuates and then calls the individual to responsibility.

What we would then have is a kind of open grieving, that is extended to those whose vulnerability to climate change is greater than our own, and that opens on to a future with a sense of outrage for the death to come and that is already ours. Open grieving, as Butler (2016: 39) suggests, is intimate with outrage, and she sees here a great sociopolitical potential in outrage directed towards the suffering of distant others as it is to those close by. As environmental catastrophe progresses, having already devastated those populations considered beyond the community of Western concern, an understanding of collective death that accommodates the faltering violence faced elsewhere, that does not wait for death to come to home shores but mourns it already elsewhere, is a necessary corrective to a Western liberal concern for its own end.

As far as environmental catastrophe is concerned, we have seen the firing squad already. But this 'we're fucked / we're dead' is not a fatalism, at least not if it is on guard against individualism and massification: on the one hand, alive to the risk that the unsteady but persistent deaths of others as a result of climate change are dismissed as individual tragedies and no more; on the other, alert to the danger of sudden, dramatic losses written off as the death of a 'they' without individual meaning or collective responsibility. This sociological vigilance is aided by an understanding of finitude as a limit that forms a community above and beyond its realization of individual identities and projects. It is only by rejecting the individualism of death – the idea that death is mine alone – that we can then mobilize concepts such as existential marginalization or existential exhaustion, concepts that will be vital for understanding the moral experience of the Anthropocene. The experience of marginalization would then be of the difficulty of imagining a future for others, for humanity, and the experience of exhaustion then the relentless stress of worrying about the death of the other as well as my own – because of my own. Such an understanding of finitude would cast death as a community-forming limitation, as something that both threatens and organizes collective possibilities before it can ever be constitutive of an individual identity. An anticipation of collective death means that 'we're fucked / we're dead' is not a nihilistic retreat but an opening onto responsibility, to being for others and not being towards death.

Radical contingency

By emphasizing the 'we' of 'we're fucked' the possibility of responsibility is opened but a further question is raised: 'we're fucked'– but says who? Who gets to speak of this fate for all the others? This is a question made more acute if we consider the difficulty of speaking of something as cataclysmic or excessive as environmental catastrophe. Derrida (2007), for example, argues that any such event is fundamentally unsayable. That is, 'if there is an event, it must never be something that is predicted or planned, or ever really decided upon' (Derrida, 2007: 441). Saying the event is impossible until its end, since the act of saying it at any point before then delimits its possibility, encapsulates the horizon of what might occur or what it might achieve. 'A predicted event', says Derrida (2007: 451), 'is not an event'. Jean-François Lyotard applies this kind of thinking to environmental catastrophe, albeit, in his case, the destruction of the earth by the heat death of the sun. He writes that such events are unsayable because they are unthinkable, that 'it's impossible to think an end, pure and simple, of anything at all, since the end's a limit and to think it you have to be on both sides of that limit' and that, after an apocalyptic event, 'there won't be a thought to know that its death took place' (Lyotard, 2004: 9). Both of these 'theorists of the cataclysm' (Clark, 2010: 46) grapple with radical contingency: the possibility that something might happen that is so radical that it is unsayable or unthinkable.

The statement 'we're fucked', then, is qualified by the indeterminacy of an event that can be anticipated but never quite grasped or articulated. That is, the catastrophe is so excessive that it is impossible to imagine there is anything we can do to avoid it, but it is also so excessive that our failure to grasp it opens the horizon of possibilities, that it forces us towards a beyond, beyond the narrow limitation of what thought presently has to achieve – to survive. This can be articulated as: 'we're fucked – as far as I know'.

Blanchot exemplifies this manner of approaching catastrophe in *The Writing of the Disaster* (1995). He writes that the disaster is infinite and always out of reach, that it is not something that lies in the future because it is the possibility that nothing else will come – that there is no future. 'To think the disaster', Blanchot (1995: 1) says, 'is to have no longer any future in which to think it'. The greatest risk of such a catastrophe is the passivity it brings; if it does not open onto any kind of future, then it holds nothing for us, given that there would be no-one left to experience it fully, that it diminishes and then ends all experience. Such an event does not put my existence into question because it rejects the question of my existence. But this does not mean that there is nothing for it. Our fear of the disaster, Blanchot (1995: 36) claims, is at heart a fear that everything already established is destroyed, when changing what is established might just be the best way of confronting the event. The disaster forces us to rethink what is acceptable and unacceptable to thought, to become uncomfortable in the face of this terrifying cataclysm and then to be more accepting of things that previously we were uncomfortable thinking. It makes impossible our masquerading in the present.

More than this, to confront the disaster, which is to say to speak of the disaster in a way that allows us to confront it, we need the language of alterity, of the other. Blanchot (1995: 114) argues that whatever escapes what can be said absolutely must be spoken of, that 'the unspeakable would be circumscribed by Speaking raised to infinity'. Here we see a distinction between *the said* and *saying* that is found also in the work of Levinas (2008b), where the said picks out what is already established and that which is inward, while saying opens onto the exterior and to a future that is nevertheless unforeseeable. Saying here might best be understood as a kind of heterology as found in the work of Georges Bataille (1985), as an act of communicating excess or incommensurability, communicating with the excessive and the incommensurable. Saying gives us back the future by acknowledging that we can no longer have the present. That is, the event is only unsayable (as per Derrida) to the extent that we attempt to understand it according to what is already acceptable to thought; go beyond this, and towards the unknowable, and something radically different can happen. We fear the radical contingency of the event when instead it presents the opportunity to speak of change and to think otherwise than disaster.

While Quentin Meillassoux (2020) has argued, as part of his rejection of the post-Kantian tradition, that we need to think a world without thought, and that science or mathematics provide the means to do so, the motivating force to knowledge in this context must, at least to some extent, be affective. Even the most likely predictions based on the most accurate climate data lack something of the absolute horror, of the existential terror and the experiential suffering of the environmental catastrophe that progresses (see Last, 2013). Kathryn Yusoff (2009) has used Blanchot (and Bataille) to explore the question of knowledge and climate change, arguing that climate change data present us with certainties but hide the excesses of the catastrophe, that they lack the sheer stalking force of the event itself. She develops the idea of excess as a form of non-knowledge, that the excessive challenges knowledge and established ethics, and that non-knowledge is not simply accepting that we do not know but recognizing what we exclude from knowledge. Yusoff argues that our awareness of the catastrophe posed by climate change should demand a radical rethinking of how we act, but instead we resist the event in order to avoid the risk of thinking anew and go about our business as usual. As such, we abandon any moral relation to what knowledge we have; and unless we are changed by that knowledge, then our anticipation of environmental catastrophe is useless.

But by what mechanism are we changed by our relationship to knowledge? Mann and Wainwright (2018: 130) suggest that 'thoughtful speculation' is preferable to 'abandoning ourselves to nihilism ("we're fucked")' or falling into visions of dystopia. It is tempting to counter that 'we're fucked' is rather a healthy dose of scepticism; not a scepticism about climate change (quite the opposite) but about humanity and its desire to respond – to survive. Blanchot (1995: 76) writes that scepticism 'is not simply nihilist negation' but a mode of approach that is uninterested in both negation and affirmation, and is, as such, neutral. It would, however, be a stretch to apply this here. Even when qualified, the statement is both negative and affirmative at once: 'we're fucked' (negation) 'as far as I know' (affirmation). It cannot be neutral.

Instead, it is possible to think of this utterance as the performance of a peculiar kind of narcissism that rejects nihilism because it embraces both hope and despair. This is not the liberal narcissism of those privileged parts of the world that have now caught up with the catastrophe, but an altogether more responsible narcissism. Derrida (2004: 199) argues that there 'is not narcissism and non-narcissism; there are narcissisms that are more or less comprehensive, generous, open, extended'. That is, there is a measure of narcissism or self-love that is necessary for altruism or love for others. 'What is called non-narcissism', says Derrida (2004: 199), 'is in general but the economy of a much more welcoming, hospitable narcissism, one that is much more open to the experience of the other as other'. This is an idea taken up by Blanchot, who argues that there is no other game in town: 'All the positions of being are narcissistic, and not-being' (1995: 125). He suggests that the part of the myth of Narcissus that has largely been forgotten is that Narcissus does not recognize himself in the reflection that so captivates him. As such, Narcissus does not see a 'doubled Same' but 'the Other within the Same' (Blanchot, 1995: 134). On the one hand, this points to a divided self that can be made or unmade in the image returned to it, and, on the other, the way that our self-regard is always interrupted by the other – that it already presupposes this other person who demands my attention.

In this context, 'we're fucked – as far as I know' evokes an individual uncertainty but also a collective consequence; as well as the threat of negation there is also affirmation, that it is only so far as I know, that I am part of a community that invigorates me but that is more than me. My limited perspective, my smallness in the face of the excessive, opens on to a movement towards community – to the other, and what is more than me – and from here society and its organization can be made or unmade, and another future welcomed. The 'I' wants to be part of the 'we' – this is its narcissism – and to continue this into a future cast in doubt by the radical contingency of environmental catastrophe, it has to embrace the radical contingency of being with others. Environmental catastrophe can be anticipated but not presently comprehended because it is monstrous, but also because the changes it demands we make to our ways of living are themselves resistant to established ways of thinking. Whoever states that 'we're fucked' faces catastrophe as a radical contingency but does so by speaking of a collective that it cannot speak for, and so the space of doubt is made open to possibilities beyond the individual. Such a position is neither nihilism nor narcissistic melancholy but the responsible narcissism of an individual that wants to be part of a community that endures.

Radical responsibility

A sociology of the very worst not only emphasizes the radical contingency of events but also of sociality. Social existence cannot be choreographed or without risk; the movement towards the other is a leap across a chasm. Our responsibility lies in responding to another without knowing how they in turn will respond. As such, the moral experience that grounds sociality is another radical contingency.

Bonneuil and Fressoz (2017: xiii) recognize the urgency of a 'revolution in morality and thought'. But is this possibility not included already in the statement 'we're fucked'? Only rarely might it be 'we're fucked (and nothing else)' since something nevertheless happens next. Instead: 'we're fucked (and so)'. In this configuration the *and* designates acceptance of this catastrophe; and the *and so* picks out the hope that there is the possibility of another future or at least the possibility of response. The *and so* held in parenthesis warns that the statement is complete without it, that without action there is only the starkest 'we're fucked'; and the omission of a question mark appended to the *so* indicates the way that the enactment of what might happen next is not a question asked of others, but a responsibility to be assumed *with* others.

The anticipation of an environmental catastrophe that is also already here is a fundamentally humbling experience to the extent that it surpasses what thought can grasp. The idea that 'we're fucked' comes from a position of humility so great that the individual can only remake themselves through an outward trajectory towards others consummated in attention and care, such that the statement opens on to a future of activity and of possibility. This rests on an understanding of responsibility that is animated by a narcissistic humility in the face of the transcendent that then becomes an enthusiasm for care and attention to the other, an enthusiasm to hold in abeyance the very worst that can happen – the death of the other. We find a feeling of humility in the face of something that transcends the individual; this humility is brought about by something that goes beyond reasoned thought and is then discharged as an enthusiasm for this other existence; and then something has to happen right at the moment when working out what it would be is most difficult (see Hill, 2019a). Moral gravity is then both the seriousness of the other's suffering that generates humility and the orientation of existence towards the other in the gesture of enthusiasm.

This understanding of the graveness and the seismic movement of moral existence finds its fullest realization in the work of Levinas and his account of the 'ethical event of sociality' (2007: 207; for a political account of enthusiasm see Lyotard, 2009). An idea of transcendence as exteriority is central to this work, that there is something beyond the 'I' or outside the subject that resists my comprehension or 'escapes my grasp' (Levinas, 2007: 39). Levinas identifies this with the other person – a transcendent other who is beyond what I can think. This other can never become a possession of my thought, fully worked out in my thinking, but instead 'withdraws into mystery' (Levinas, 2008d: 86). This is encapsulated by the idea of 'the stranger in the neighbour' (Levinas, 2008b: 123), where proximity is bound up with an impassable distance. But while I cannot comprehend this other fully, the other speaks to me and reveals my responsibility. The other then obligates me to respond from above and below – a 'destitute authority', as Amit Pinchevski (2005: 217) characterizes it – and so this encounter with transcendence is also something concrete to the extent that it is a response. Levinas (2008b: 53) argues that the encounter with the other is experienced as a call to help, a call for care and attention, a call that picks me out as someone and not anyone, me who 'in the absence of anyone is called up to be someone, and cannot step away from this call'. And in responding, I make myself vulnerable, I expose myself to the other. 'This exposure', says Levinas (2008b: 15), 'is the frankness, sincerity, veracity of saying'; not a response 'protecting itself in the said' but 'uncovering itself' or 'offering itself even in suffering'. I am called before all others to expose myself in the face of the unknown, to risk myself for the other – to give at all costs.

This then forms a 'relation without relation' (Levinas, 2007: 80), the bond without a bond Derrida identified in the instant of Blanchot's death. It is a 'relation with a reality infinitely distant from my own reality, yet without this distance destroying this relation and without this relation destroying this distance' (Levinas, 2007: 41). We do not form a totality; the other remains transcendent, always steps away, and my responsibility, once moved, is always to move towards. Levinas (2006b: 88) defines this relationship as 'responsibility for my neighbour', which he says is simply 'the harsh name for what we call love for the neighbour'. 'This sociality is not an experience of the other', Levinas explains to Lyotard, at the conclusion of a debate on knowledge, and by way of summary here; 'it is a proximity to the other. It is the love of the other, if you will, it is friendship with the other. It is the fact of not being indifferent to the death of the other' (in Lyotard, 2020: 103).

This way of understanding responsibility influences not only Blanchot's account of moral existence but also his thinking about catastrophe. In *The Writing of the Disaster* (1995) Blanchot argues that to be yourself or to be self-same is only something distinguishable in the relation to the other and yet the relation to the other is the ruination of one's identity – because it charges me with a responsibility that is not mine. Blanchot (1995: 18, emphasis in original) writes that the responsible individual becomes 'the *hostage* (as Levinas says)', the guarantor 'of a promise he hasn't made' and 'the irreplaceable one who is not in his own place'. That I am called to responsibility calls me into question, since it reveals my freedom as something that might recklessly be discharged on others, on others whose experiences I cannot share, and so discharged with consequences I cannot comprehend. Blanchot explains: 'If the Other calls me into question to the point of stripping me of myself, it is because he is himself absolute nakedness, the entreaty which disqualifies the me in me till it becomes sheer torture' (1995: 22–3). (Nudity is often used by Levinas to evoke the vulnerability of the other; see, for example, Levinas, 2007: 75.) In the encounter I am interrupted and undone by the other, and then remade otherwise when I orient myself outwards in the gesture of responsibility.

Blanchot (1995: 25) says that Levinas has transformed the meaning of 'responsibility' from the dutiful act of the conscientious individual to the requirement to face up to the impossibility of being responsible. Responsibility becomes an orientation away from the self in response to the impossible task of ever giving enough or loving enough. There is then humility, a self humbled by its being called into question and humbled again by the task it cannot hope to complete. And there is nevertheless enthusiasm for this task. In *The Instant of my Death* (2000: 5) Blanchot writes that the young man before the firing squad felt 'a sort of beatitude (nothing happy however)'. Nothing happy but a blessedness, a blissfulness. Why? Blanchot (2000: 5) continues, and we have seen this before: 'Perhaps ecstasy. Rather the feeling of the compassion for suffering humanity, the happiness of not being immortal or eternal.' Nothing happy but a self-transcendence and then, rather, a moral relationship, of compassion and the rejection of indifference to the other's mortality. This 'rather' that transforms self-transcendence (ecstasy), on its own perhaps an egoistic narcissism, into an outward movement of care, captures the moment of enthusiasm. Nothing happy but an enthusiasm for responsibility.

We see the humility-enthusiasm experience of moral existence play out in Blanchot's framing of the disaster as infinite – as something always out of reach. In the face of this disaster the individual feels 'anonymous and bereft of self' (Blanchot, 1995: 14); if it is out of my reach, beyond me, if I cannot grasp it then it offers nothing for me, nothing that might define me. Blanchot (1995: 1) writes that the 'disaster ruins everything' but 'does not touch anyone in particular', that

' "I" am not threatened by it, but spared, left aside', and that 'it is in this way that the disaster threatens in me that which is exterior to me'. This then is our humility, to understand that the disaster will not happen to me because I will not be there when it arrives, but that it destroys everything outside me, outside the subject, and with it the exteriority that gives any coherence to my interiority, my self-sameness. And so, then, and again, there is enthusiasm.

The 'and so' operates in the space between the catastrophe having arrived and it still being to come, a space in which something must be done (if anything can be done). Here is our responsibility as an anticipation of catastrophe manifest as an ethical sociality, as attention and care, an exposure, to humble oneself. To assume this responsibility before all others would be a narcissistic humility, not simply because it calls me above all but because it allows for the situation of the 'I' in a 'we', in a collective where both might flourish: the 'I' because its hypostatic identity is ruined, as Blanchot has it, but a new decentred mode of existence is found in the trajectory towards the other; and the other as the recipient of care and attention. In such a collective, the death of the other is the very worst thing that can happen because when my death comes, I am not there; when it comes to the other, I was already responsible for keeping it at bay, however forlorn it is to be charged with such a responsibility. We anticipate the disaster only through our enthusiasm for the other – our love, our friendship, our refusal of indifference to their death.

Despite everything, despite climate change and the possibility that everything might become impossible in some unthinkable end, this movement towards the other is a movement towards the future; that is, if we want to have any enthusiasm for the future and not just despondency about the unfolding of a cataclysm, it can only be through our enthusiasm for the other. It is risky, but then it must be. I am undone by it, but then so must everything be. Our vulnerability to climate change, whether sudden lurches of loss or a faltering but nevertheless collective death, connects us to the vulnerability of the body of the other. Assuming responsibility for this vulnerability is a necessary condition if we want there to be a future in which human life is possible, even if, in the final reckoning, it is not enough. In saying 'we're fucked (and so)' the possibility of avoiding the starkest and unqualified realization of 'we're fucked' is acknowledged. But only as non-indifference, attention, care; only as recognition of the class interests of despairing populations; only through a responsibility that responds to the radically contingent with a moral movement that is itself radical and contingent – that risks everything for everything.

We're fucked

The statement 'we're fucked' expresses an existential condition that cannot be reduced to fatalism or dismissed as nihilism. It might mean 'we're fucked / we're dead', that there is a death that threatens the collective before it can ever threaten the individual, and that therefore locates the problem as something that can only be faced collectively. This 'we're fucked' presupposes community. It must mean 'we're fucked – as far as I know', since it is impossible to speak of the catastrophe with certainty and to speak for the collective without such speech encountering alterity. This 'we're fucked' then acknowledges a community that is heterologous. And it should mean 'we're fucked (and so)', which is to say that something must happen next, at this moment that the catastrophe threatens everything, that it humbles me, and this something is an enthusiasm for the other as an orientation to the future. This 'we're fucked' demands a moral community. In each instance the possibility of hope emerges from a statement of despair and builds sequentially to the hope that a different future is possible. This critical pessimism is limited: it does not speak of this future or even really set us on its path. But it prepares us for this journey. It holds in mind the right kind of death, which is to say the worst kind of death, the death of the other; it acknowledges the unspeakable horror of the catastrophe, and what cannot be said, and demands a response; and above everything, in facing the very worst it centres what might be the very best of life here on our warming earth: care and attention for those we share it with. There are other ways of motivating responsibility, but this approach finds it even at the point that we might just give up on everything.

By understanding the experience of finitude as a collectivizing event, such that being is not oriented towards one's death but the other, we can better understand the marginalization and exhaustion that attend our social condition as we confront environmental catastrophe. An understanding of our relationship to death as a community-forming limit, before it can be an identity-forming limit, only sharpens our social criticism of the murderous abandonment of distant others to deracinating floods and uninhabitable heat. By locating this catastrophe at the heart of the social, because our present society is best understood in relation to the very worst that it makes possible, we can begin to grasp the scale of change necessary to avoid devastation. To anticipate the disaster, even when its manifestation escapes what we might imagine, and to recognize this radical contingency in the very formation of our social condition, the way that the individual is ruined and then imperilled but finally emboldened by sociality, we can better articulate a sense of responsibility adequate to the task of confronting the catastrophe presented to us by climate change. An account of social existence that acknowledges the humility of the individual in the face of the transcendent, and that emphasizes the importance of turning this humility into enthusiasm for others, would then put material response at the heart of its conceptual activism.

This critical pessimism is not a fatalism or a nihilism but the working of a sociological imagination that looks despairingly in search for hope. It would be both an outraged mourning of the dispossessed and a call to an environmentalism of precarious lives. This pessimism anticipates the very worst (death, catastrophe, anonymity, incoherence, undoing) because such conditions reveal something fundamental about our social existence, and when we work from fundamentals, from a position of primordial sociality, perhaps anything is possible.

And then, finally, the utility of thinking of the very worst would lie in its not coming to pass.

TWO

Exodus

If the cause of pessimism can be advanced, then the threat of false hope still dogs our orientation to the future. According to the Intergovernmental Panel on Climate Change (IPCC, 2019), a quarter of the ice-free surface of the earth is subject to anthropogenic degradation: soil erosion from agriculture far outstrips the soil formation rate; the area of drylands in drought is increasing; and around 500 million people now live in areas that have experienced desertification since the 1980s. The catastrophe stretches its legs. Holly Buck (2019) worries that there will come a point when we give up hope, and while we have seen that all is not lost when we accept that we have fucked it all, her subsequent concern for how hopelessness will be leapt upon by opportunism is something that needs to be addressed. At our lowest point, she suggests, we become less resistant to the technological solutionism of, for example, solar engineering, where sunlight would be diverted into space, changing the reflectivity of the earth to arrest its warming.

These kinds of planetary interventions reveal what was always there: that environmental catastrophe and our approaches to it are social and not simply technoscientific matters. Félix Guattari (2018: 17–18) argued that we have to confront environmental catastrophe as a problem that is not distinct from questions of social relation and human subjectivity such that, ultimately, the question is not only of industrial pollution, but also, more broadly, of our ways of being on the planet. This approach is sustained by Paul Virilio (2005a: 124–5), who imagines an ecology constituted by the earthly, the corporeal and the intersubjective, and bound together by gravity. Gravity – as the seriousness of existence – binds the animal body *to* the terrestrial body and *in* the social body.

But what if we could break free of this gravity and leave behind the catastrophe to come? This is the vision of two tech entrepreneurs and their respective aerospace companies: Elon Musk, co-founder of PayPal and CEO of Tesla, who incorporated SpaceX in 2002; and Jeff Bezos, the Amazon billionaire, who founded Blue Origin in 2000. Through innovative and disruptive practices, SpaceX and Blue Origin are positioned today as powerful players not only in the aerospace industry, but also in the move to push industry and commercial enterprise into space. Both men now want to use these advances to address the environmental devastation of our planet (see Davenport, 2018; Fernholz, 2018). For Musk, the best way to survive environmental catastrophe will be to colonize Mars, to the extent that he has claimed that everything that SpaceX achieves in the aerospace industry is part of a project to prove that a self-sustaining city on the red planet is not only possible, but it will also be thriving within 40 to 100 years of the first manned flight there. This, he announced at the International Astronautical Congress in 2016, would, by setting humans up as an interplanetary species, ensure that a backup planet is available to sustain human populations when conditions on earth become uninhabitable. Bezos takes a slightly different line. If industrial activity is destroying the planet, he avers, then the solution is not simply to move the people to another planet, but to move the industrial activity, along with all its pollution and degradation, into space. That way, the earth could be regreened and preserved as a kind of national park on a global scale. Both plans might be characterized as a kind of *green exodus*, removing human activity from the earth either as a reaction or solution to environmental catastrophe.

Assuming the very worst, we must address what it might mean to leave the earth behind, how we might fare as a society in space, and take in hand this drive to take the human beyond our planet. Such an undertaking is vital for a radical reimagining of moral responsibility and solidarity. Any escape from earth would transplant the human into an environment so alien that the experience of human existence would be irrevocably altered, losing not only the physical ground of human activity but also the weight of social co-habitation; contemplating such an exodus would then direct us to what matters here on earth. In any event, the question is not so much whether the colonization of Mars is possible, in some technical sense, but whether it is possible to remove the human body from the terrestrial body without losing the heart of the social body – the moral gravity that binds us all.

Green exodus

These visions of leaving the planet and colonizing Mars are not so much a form of environmental futurology as they are an attempt to neutralize the threat of the future in order to justify the persistence of growth. The idea of a green exodus, pushed by those whose capitalization of digital infrastructure has contributed to the environmental catastrophe it seeks to sidestep, is a mask for a risk management exercise wedded to continued development.

Musk and Bezos have risen to a position to shape visions of off-planet existence through fortunes made in the digital economy (see Davenport, 2018; Fernholz, 2018). Musk made his name by co-founding PayPal, having been involved in companies developing online payment systems through the 1990s. His wealth and corporate power, then, are intimately bound up with the financial infrastructure of the internet, the proceeds from which allowed him to develop SpaceX – as well as the electric car and renewable energy company Tesla. Bezos's corporate identity is closely associated with Amazon, the online retailer founded in 1994. Amazon has grown to become much more than an e-commerce company, branching out into logistics, cloud computing, consumer electronics and so on (see Hill, 2020b; Hill, 2021). Blue Origin's business model was based on the acceptance that it was not going to make any money in the short to medium term, relying instead on Bezos's capital to allow it to compete. Bezos's superior wealth has meant that Blue Origin has been less reliant on government contracts than SpaceX, although Musk has been boosted by investment from Peter Thiel (co-founder of PayPal) and the purchase of 10 per cent of SpaceX by Google in 2015 for US$1 billion. As it happens, Google executives Larry Page and Eric Schmidt have invested in Planetary Resources, a company planning to mine asteroids for precious metals. Whether it is by the method of payment, the means to distribute goods or the organization of data, the wealth of the digital economy has been a significant catalyst for the commercialization of space in its present form. Musk and Bezos were able to use this wealth to disrupt the hold of the state on space travel – and both source and application provide a curious platform for their environmental problem-solving.

It is tempting to think of digital media as clean or ethereal, but they are deeply implicated in our environmental catastrophe. Our personal electronic devices may be largely mobile, giving the appearance of ethereality, or an untethering from the world, but their batteries are still charged by electricity in the main produced by burning fossil fuels (Cubitt, 2017). Data processing is energy intensive and creates huge amounts of heat (Parikka, 2015: 24), with 20 per cent of the energy used by server farms put to work cooling the servers (Cubitt, 2017: 19–20). The growth in cloud computing between 2012 and 2015 led to an increased carbon footprint from 6 megatonnes of CO_2 to 30 – equivalent to putting 4.9 million cars on the road (Lewis, 2017: 59). This demand for energy is matched by a demand for materials and minerals. Cobalt to make tantalum capacitors for digital technologies is mined in conflict zones like the Democratic Republic of Congo, where child slaves are put to work in dangerous conditions (Qiu, 2016: 22); tin for solder is mined in Indonesia, where the water table is fouled and the coral reef destroyed by mine runoff (Greenfield, 2017: 19); lithium is extracted for batteries from the salt lakes of Bolivia, Chile and Argentina, polluting wildlife habitats and commodifying water in drought conditions (Cubitt, 2017: 64–9). This is not to mention the energy used in producing digital technologies in the first place, often in regions reliant on coal-based energy (Parikka, 2015: 99); or the emissions cost of global freight every time we buy things online (with PayPal or through Amazon, say) (Cubitt, 2017: 102); or the toxicity of the e-waste generated through cycles of consumption and obsolescence (Parikka, 2015: 141). Digital media are as much a part of the pollution of our environment as factories and mines because this is precisely where they come from – and then some. They are inextricably bound up with the finitude of the earthly and the perceived need to exceed it.

The commercialization of space is an important part of the extension of capitalism beyond the limits of the planet, and it is significant that Musk and Bezos decided to invest some of their considerable wealth in such a project. There is now a perception that government bodies such as NASA have been crowded out by private enterprise, under attack from a 'space libertarian community' who call for off-planet free markets and the opening of space flight to competition, and who see NASA as an obstacle to enterprise (Parker, 2009: 91). Musk and Bezos both saw the aerospace industry as monopolistic, heavily subsidized by the federal government in the US and in need of disruption (see Davenport, 2018; Fernholz, 2018). Musk, for example, took his complaints about the anti-competition practices of NASA to a Senate committee in order to force NASA to open up its bidding process, and went as far as suing the United States Air Force for the right to compete for Pentagon launch contracts. Musk in particular was disdainful of what he saw as a lack of desire to make a business out of space exploration, believing NASA to be too risk averse to engage with projects that might fail, and blind to the fact that such failure would drive innovation – even the acceleration of progress.

Both men have been part of the move to disrupt the aerospace industry, shifting it from cost-plus to competitive fixed-cost contract bidding, and bringing any number of innovations – from vertical take-off and landing to reusable rockets. This attention to saving costs has been matched by a preoccupation with saving time – finding innovative ways to bring innovations to market quicker – that has then merged with visions of saving the planet. For example, Blue Origin's coat of arms features a winged hourglass, symbolizing not only the heavenly status of efficiency savings but also time slipping away before a need to take flight from the environmental devastation of our planet. Bezos is adamant that at Blue Origin it is always *Day 1* (which is also the name of the Amazon HQ building in Seattle, Washington). In 2017 he wrote: 'Day 2 is stasis. Followed by irrelevance. Followed by excruciating, painful decline. Followed by death. And *that* is why it is *always* Day 1' (in Davenport, 2018: 75, emphasis in original). What Bezos is describing here is given the heroic status of a struggle against finitude, but it is essentially just a paean to unmitigated growth. An adherence to the ideology of endless growth and accumulation is unlikely to make our continued presence on the planet more viable – something already borne out by Musk and Bezos's successes in the digital economy.

Both men have risen to a position where their proclamations on the future of humanity are taken seriously because they put capital first. They are, as such, unlikely, in the final reckoning, to suddenly put the future of humanity ahead of the growth of capital. The same reckless adherence to growth and development that has reaped such gargantuan profits in the tech industry is applied to their rocketeering. Talk of a green exodus rarely acknowledges the heavy emissions contribution and waste production of the space industry (Ormrod, 2013: 737) – not to mention the rapaciousness of colonization. The idea that the colonization of space might be an adequate response to environmental catastrophe is somewhat undermined by the desire to exploit the natural resources found on other planets, moons and asteroids. Space has already been littered with technological waste – satellites and probes and so on (see Damjanov, 2015) – and now technology companies are set on repeating the excesses of industrial exploitation beyond the earth's orbit.

Blue Origin see the moon as their first port of call because it is here possible to extract water and make rocket propellant off-world, extending the range of their spacecrafts and minimizing the amount of weight that needs to be taken to escape velocity to break free of the earth's gravity (Fernholz, 2018: 241). This would pave the way for a more expansive resource extraction in space, the first stage of a land grab as corporations compete for chemical and mineral resources. As Peter Dickens (2009: 68) argues, the political and economic energy invested in exploiting off-planet resources misdirects that needed to deal with inequalities and crises on earth. While the problem of environmental catastrophe is held in common, its impacts are not shared out evenly. This is the double tap of colonialism: to extract and exploit and pollute; to make lives precarious in this extraction and exploitation and pollution; and to then abandon those populations to the choking smogs and violent storms and rising seas as the catastrophe they always lived in extends to those who profited from it. Those with the least will be hit first and hit worst. But because of this inequality, not all people are equally placed to respond to the crisis, and so the technological fixes of the wealthy dominate our visions of the future. Green exodus not only continues the human activity that led us to our existential crisis, only out there in space, it ignores the particularities of that crisis as they unfold at local levels here on earth.

At its heart, the idea of a green exodus aims at the legitimation of social and political institutions and practices, ways of thinking, and ways of being, that are bound up with the ideology of development, as endless growth and accumulation, and it does so by postulating a future that ought to be accomplished – or rather an idea that needs to be realized. This is an idea of a homogenized humanity-as-cargo that can simply be lifted from the planet and placed elsewhere, inequalities and reckless behaviours intact. At its heart, then, is a totalizing tendency that seeks to control the unexpected by recourse to the already tried and tested, and it is successful because it emanates from personifications of capital whose prescriptions are permitted to become norms that obligate others. With their visions of more of the same, only in space, Musk and Bezos are in the business of managing risk and neutralizing the future, rather than envisioning something better. And, since risk is seen as something 'out there' that can be located and captured – and exploited – they go about business as usual, while the ideology that underpins their activities goes on undisturbed.

Framing environmental catastrophe as a risk rather than as a tragedy makes it viable to seek market solutions rather than to approach its unfolding as a call to an unprecedented moral response. To locate what is happening within the purview of risk management is a political move, since it then delimits what can be done and nominates who can or ought to do it, while the consequences of these actions hit those excluded from the decision-making power unequally (see Wright and Nyberg, 2015: 48–9). Men like Musk and Bezos are permitted to confront the risk without bearing its brunt, while the solutions the market permits are incapable of addressing the unequal experiences of climate change and pollution. And all the while, the science fiction gloss of a green exodus tells us that everything is fine, that we can have more growth, that development is a viable logic, but that it just needs a new home.

Grey exodus

We are left not with a *green* but – and taking inspiration here from Paul Virilio – a *grey exodus*. Given the context – the drive towards taking humans off the planet in the face of catastrophe – a turn to the work of Jean-François Lyotard here would make sense, since his book *The Inhuman* (2004) contains an essay on just such a scenario. The argument that runs through this text is that human culture is unsuitable for transplantation beyond the surface of the earth, since it is sustained and nurtured by specific contexts and conditions that are not easily replicated or transmitted, in part because what it means to be human would have to be so augmented by technology to survive extraterrestrially that it would not endure the relocation. Virilio (in Virilio and Lotringer, 2002: 119) picks up on this text, which he characterizes as Lyotard's attempt to grapple with 'the idea of the cosmonaut', of the body that needs to mutate to survive, but he also appears to dismiss it in a cursory way as a text on cyborg modification that is remiss in not situating the problem within ecology. Such a reading seems ungenerous.

Underpinning Lyotard's work here is an argument that technoscientific development is wedded to the advance of the system of capital; that this system innovates itself to overcome obstacles to its advance (in his essay a solar apocalypse but also, perhaps, more immediate environmental catastrophe); and that the overcoming of these obstacles is not only unaligned with human interest but also rests on the abandonment of whole populations. There is here, then, a useful critique of the ideology of development that motivates the tech entrepreneurs and their dreams of Mars. There is also a certain sympathy here with the ecological thinking of Virilio (and Guattari before him), even if Virilio himself did not recognize it, but the turn to Virilio and not to Lyotard, in this instance, is motivated by the different ways that they frame what is lost if the human – or what might be left of the human – is plucked from the earth. Lyotard's argument is motivated by the fear that we will lose human difference, especially gendered difference and, therefore, desire. Virilio instead focuses on the loss of human experience (the lifeworld), and this emphasis, it is contended, provides a fruitful platform for a critique of green exodus that also takes account of its homogenizing and exclusionary effect.

Virilio was concerned about space travel as part of a broader critique of the impact of technoscientific development and speed on both the individual and the social body. Development is often presented as a kind of progress to sell technological or scientific advances or solutions as the flourishing of humanity and, therefore, as a moral good. Virilio (2005b: 1) argues instead that technoscientific development is not measured in progress but in its relationship to catastrophe. That is, the success of the system is determined by its ability to proceed beyond limit-situations (such as environmental catastrophe) and not by its facilitation of human betterment. Speed becomes an important dimension of the maintenance and extension of the system, even if it adds little in itself to human flourishing. In fact, 'far from aggrandising the individual', Virilio (2005a: 124) suggests, 'progress in technology diminishes him, makes him smaller, to the point of shortly triggering his physiological desertification – which is another way of saying his emptiness, his uselessness'. We are left with pure, naked speed in service of the 'delirious logic' (Virilio, 1996b: 30) of constant growth.

This high-speed pursuit of endless development leaves us facing two distinct but interrelated ecological crises: the first, through the risk of climate change and the threat of environmental catastrophe, falls under *green ecology*; the second, the deleterious impact of the speed of development on the depth of field of our environment, is what Virilio refers to as *grey ecology*. The latter encompasses the pollution of distance and time, the diminishment of the life-size and 'the degradation of the expanse of our habitat' (Virilio, 2008b: 58). This is a kind of pollution, then, that strikes not at the breathability of our air or the fecundity of our soil or the levels of our seas, but at our perception of the social environment and, therefore, our experience of the others that occupy it. Grey ecology takes its name from the way that the pursuit of speed as the driving force of development overwhelms human concern, both as a project and as an affective act; as Mark Featherstone (2008: 197) explains, the effects of speed 'cause the colours of human diversity to merge into the amoral murk of greyness', and so we lose the brilliance, the vitality of what it is to be human. Virilio (1990: 89) concludes that 'the most important ecological struggles', grey or green, 'have all taken place and been organized around the problem of speed'. The pursuit of speed pollutes the natural environment while its accomplishment derogates the human experience.

Musk and Bezos made their money through speed – of data, of communication, of transaction. As Virilio (in Virilio and Lotringer, 1997: 35–6) argues, the wealth part of this equation is usually taken seriously but not the role of speed itself: 'Wealth is the hidden side of speed and speed the hidden side of wealth. The two form an absolute couple.' This political economy of speed underpins much of Virilio's critique of technology and science – and militarization, urbanization and society in general – but it receives marked attention in his writings on the space industry. Here Virilio (2008a: 143) argues that escape velocity in particular – the acceleration that is required to escape the earth's gravity, approximately 11,200 metres a second – 'becomes the equivalent of profit'. In the space industry acceleration exceeds even accumulation – and its accomplishment alters what it means to be human. Below the escape velocity, as Virilio (2008b: 31) notes, all speeds are affected by the earth's pull, including the speed of perception, and, therefore, of our experience and interaction of and within the world's landscape. Achieving orbit or reaching beyond – to the moon or to Mars – 'can only be achieved by overcoming the constant imposed by the force of gravity' (Virilio, 2008b: 32). Under this constant, the trajectories of earthly things remain within the grounded experience of the everyday; beyond it – a different 'trajectography' (Virilio, 2008b: 129). Trajectography, in the work of Virilio, picks out spaces of human activity in terms of movement or orientation. Outer space, then, represents an environment where perception is disrupted, altered to the extent that we are no longer oriented, perhaps at all but at least no longer as we were.

Achieving orbit might be a triumph of escape over pull, but objects in orbit are still essentially falling in a circle, the force of gravity only offset by lateral momentum. But beyond orbit, Virilio (2008b: 67–8) argues, as we take flight from this world, we are still falling; not back to earth, but this time into a world with which we have no relationship, of which we have no experience. This is a world where there are no human dimensions: 'Beyond the boundaries of our biosphere', writes Virilio (1996a: 109, emphasis in original), 'there are indeed no *dimensions* worthy of the name: no more height, breadth, or depth, no yesterday and no tomorrow, only light-years'. This is a radically new trajectography that disorients the human. Gaining escape velocity is not only to free ourselves of geography, but also from our experience of solid ground; we 'lose our bearings' (Virilio, 2008b: 132). For Virilio, this lost ground is the anchor of intersubjectivity – where the animal body is situated in the social body – and by losing our bearings, we lose our orientation towards one another, the social glue or moral gravity of our shared existence. If we lose the place and the temporality of the earthly then we lose the dimensions of our being together. This, for Virilio, is a question of grey ecology: 'The conquest of space is also a decorporealisation of the body, the earth's body and the human body, the world proper and the body proper' (in Virilio and Lotringer, 2002: 119). As Douglas Kellner (1999: 110–11) explains, astronauts are, for Virilio, 'harbingers of a new experience beyond the familiar space and time coordinates of material existence'. Space then becomes a non-place, governed by the speed of light, that is disorienting because it rids us of the weight of human existence. In the end, Virilio (1999: 88) suggests that the very idea of such an exodus is unviable: 'The fantasy of the beyond Earth is its annihilation.'

If we are compelled to flee the desertification of the surface of our planet described by the IPCC, we had better make sure that the promised land beyond the earth's gravity is not itself a desert. Virilio (2005a: 113) uses 'desertification' to refer to the shrinking of the world by the speed of technology, or, as Featherstone (2003: 435) puts it, 'the mortification ... of the phenomenological life-world'. A desert is a kind of 'pure surface' without any relief (Virilio, 2008a: 131). It is a space in which the obstacles of the world and of the body have been replaced by the flat, weightless environment of pure speed. Virilio (2005a: 114) argues that any exodus from the planet would be a 'great leap into the void of celestial nothingness' that leads us to a new desert: 'the vastness of the cosmic void'. Rather than a green exodus as a sustainable plan for the future of humanity, a reading of Virilio suggests instead something more like a grey exodus. That is, technoscientific development is primarily complicit with the extension and acceleration of accumulation; it will locate solutions to avoiding limit-situations that have little or no regard for human cost; and the primary casualty to this is the experience of existence. It is grey in the sense that it discolours the perception of the lifeworld and grey in the sense that it successfully obscures the fact that it has nothing whatsoever to do with human progress. In the context of an exodus to space, we might say that leaving behind the earth presents itself as a viable solution because the calculation of its effectiveness has no place for human experience; according to this logic of speed and accumulation, if we have to forgo the surface of the planet, or even what it means to be human itself, to keep the system moving forward, then so be it.

Transexodus

These plans of escape, in both conception and accomplishment, reduce human diversity to a mass to be transported, losing the multiplicity of human existence and its relationship to the other. What makes such an exodus grey is the violent separation of the concrete and the transcendent, a *transexodus* that refuses the limit-situation rather than encountering it face on.

Virilio's account of experience and existence is best understood with reference to the formative role played by Maurice Merleau-Ponty and Jean Wahl (see Hill, 2019b), although these speak through his work in different ways. For Virilio, perception is not a mental representation or the content of consciousness but a kind of bodily responsiveness. That is, his account of perception is not that of Edmund Husserl's *Ideas* (2012) but of Merleau-Ponty's *Phenomenology of Perception* (2014). Perception, then, means being familiar with and finding one's way around an environment, inhabiting a world bodily, or, being in the world. For Merleau-Ponty, an experience of a given space is shaped by the way that our bodies are already geared to the world. Perception, ultimately, is a kind of communication with the world as the place of one's life; the world questions us and we respond.

The idea of a grey exodus, then, encompasses the fear, articulated by Virilio, that outer space is so alien that it does not pose us any questions at all, or, at least, that we are unable to respond to the kinds of questions it might pose because we are not adequately geared to the environment. A body dislocated from its habitual geography and subjected to new conditions will experience its existence in new and alien ways. Given that all human existence has been conducted on the surface of the earth, it is difficult not to conclude that such an exodus would lead us back to the desert. But while Merleau-Ponty quite explicitly drives Virilio's argument in this direction, Wahl's influence is more implicit, sometimes even elusive, and capturing it extends the account of grey exodus already explicated. It is in Wahl's account of transcendence and the concrete that we can not only see what a supposedly green exodus is up to, but also precisely why it would be so detrimental to carry it out – and to so grey our experience of existence.

Peter Dickens (2009), drawing on Rosa Luxemburg's argument that capitalism always requires an outside to expand into, suggests that the commercialization of space shows imperialism on the march again. Behind the idea of a green exodus is an understanding of exteriority as something that ought to be colonized. Apart from the fact that it may not be possible to bring outer space into the human environment without losing the human altogether, this represents an unhealthy relationship with transcendence. It would bring about a state of 'bare life', in the sense developed by John Lechte (2018) in his account of Georges Bataille, as existence without transcendence. A transcendent life, Lechte says, would go towards the other and embrace exteriority. Moving the deleterious adventure of capitalist development into space would instead be an imperialism of the same. Without something beyond the human – beyond our reach, beyond our grasp, beyond our mastery – we hollow out what it means to be human. Lechte (2018: 95) suggests we become 'subjects of abandonment', which is appropriate enough in the context of planetary exodus.

While a relationship with transcendence is something to aim for, the kinds of technoscientific fixes to environmental catastrophe that aim for the stars would transcend human life itself. This is a point made in relation to climate change by Sheila Jasanoff (2010), who argues that we are led by solutions that lead us in turn to universality by abstraction, that impersonal visions of what we might do in response triumph over subjective and situated imaginaries. The result is a kind of totality. Something like a green exodus would similarly bring us a 'totalizing image of the world as it is' (Jasanoff, 2010: 236), which is to say, not even as it really is (a collection of local perspectives and actions), never mind how it could be. This flattening out in the form of totalization is what makes this kind of exodus grey. The idea that the cosmos is capitalism's outside, in the sense that it is available to expand into, stands in contrast to the cosmic terror elicited in the otherness of the cosmos, at least as described by Angela Last (2013) in her reading of Mikhail Bakhtin. Last argues that environmental catastrophe is beyond the limited imagination of human beings, and that we need in response to find a new relationship with nature, one that includes all the universe. Perhaps. What is essential is a new relationship to transcendence – or at the very least a rejection of the predatory domestication of the exterior by capital. This is made clearer by the turn to Wahl.

Wahl's phenomenology centres the concrete reality of human existence rather than the ideal (or the essences of Husserl). This includes an understanding of transcendence that does not take us out of this world but is instead fundamental to the human experience. 'Transcendence', writes Wahl (2017: 40), 'is the idea of a beyond by means of which knowledge has a direction, toward which it directs itself, from which it draws its nourishment'. This beyond is not to be found out there, but in the time and space of the everyday. This location of transcendence within the concrete forms part of Wahl's rejection of totality. The presence of transcendence means that it is not possible to enclose the sense of existence in a system, since that which is beyond will escape such systematization. Instead, the concrete world is made up of radical heterogeneities. 'There is no system of existence', says Wahl (2017: 97), in his critique of G.W.F. Hegel, because a world of universality misses so much, and when we fail to universalize, as we inevitably do, we affirm this fact – we affirm transcendence. That is, we embrace a 'world of problems, ruptures, and failures', an environment made up of difference and 'irreducible multiplicities' (Wahl, 2017: 106). Wahl calls this a relationship with exteriority or with the other.

The very idea of a green exodus ought to be questioned, not only because human existence would fare badly in conditions that would so radically alter human experience, but also because it seeks to systematize the heterogeneous and to treat multiplicities as a totality. That is, the problem is not only where such plans would take us but also where they begin from. The exodus is greyed by its constitution of humanity as a mass and by its circumvention of anxiety in the face of a limit-situation. This is made clearer by Wahl's commentaries on the existentialism of Martin Heidegger and Søren Kierkegaard. Here Wahl characterizes Heidegger's the They (das Man) as a dictatorship of the simultaneous masses, a dictatorship that thrives in the anonymity of this mass simultaneity. 'Every secret loses its force', warns Wahl (2017: 111), 'every decision, every responsibility, disappears; each passes off his responsibilities onto the contemporary crowd and onto universal history'. The They, then, is a negation of possibility, or, 'everything becomes possible, but it is an imagined possibility, a simple wish, a modality of desire and vague aspiration' (Wahl, 2017: 112). Visions of Mars imagine a They, and, in imagining it, it is constructed as an integral part of the plan for the future of humanity; that is, the humanity that is allowed to be imagined into the future is homogenous, massified. In so doing, we lose the value of diversity, the responsibility to difference, and gain in its place the appearance of a decision, the suggestion of a possibility for the endurance of human existence – when really it would be its negation. It is a panicked plan in the face of great anxiety.

In his explorations of Kierkegaard, Wahl (2017: 113) took anxiety to be an individualizing force – individuating might be a better way of framing this – that is formative to an 'I' that confronts the nothing, or, the disruption of the possible. Anxiety acts as 'a revelation of being in the world' (Wahl, 2017: 114). This is in contradistinction to the They, which affords only a cheap universality, and not the solidarity of the individuated who form a 'we' (see also Stiegler, 2009). The 'I' must choose choice; the They is the negation of choice. Visions of a green exodus construct a They so that men like Musk and Bezos get to choose what happens to all of humanity, in its multifaceted reality, now reduced to a standardized cargo for their next space mission. And all of this to escape the limit-situation of environmental catastrophe – or at least to escape the anxiety that it encourages. For Wahl, the experience of the limit-situation and existence are one and the same thing: 'to exist is to commit the sin of limitation, and to have the feeling of helplessness'

(Wahl, 2017: 141) – and in this way, we also become aware of our own freedom. But, as Wahl draws from his reading of Karl Jaspers, we cannot choose to react to the limit-situation by carrying on as before and imagining that, through this calculation, the whole thing will be overcome; instead, we must adopt a radically different kind of action. 'We become ourselves by entering into limit-situations with open eyes', says Jaspers (in Wahl, 2017: 141). We are blinded to the limit itself if we imagine that more of the same, only somewhere else, is a reasonable response to the consequences of human activity.

We have a choice. In confrontation with a world torn apart we can choose to embrace transcendence or to find false comfort in totalizing projects that represent instead an exodus from the transcendent – or *transexodus*. Wahl (2017: 157) draws a distinction between transcendence as 'transascendence' and as 'transdescendence': transascendence as a movement towards the other; and transdescendence as an immersion in the concrete. Whenever we have the one without the other, we are in trouble. Without the transcendent we fall into totality; without the concrete, we lose the ground of all experience – including that of transcendence. Wahl (2017: 161) argues that it is possible to be exceeded from below as well as from above. We need to ascend and to descend. The important thing is the movement of the transcended towards that which transcends it, the gravity of moral existence.

In the case of a green exodus, we are asked to imagine forming a totality and jettisoning the concrete to sustain human existence beyond the limit-situation of environmental catastrophe; that is, to transcend the abrupt finitude of human experience. This is unsustainable, since the moment we lose the concrete we become unanchored from the ground of experience that sustains any relationship with the transcendent; and because the very plan for such an exodus constructs a They that precludes multiplicity and difference and, above all, otherness through the totalizing function of technoscientific solutionism and its flattening out of local and perspectival experiences of climate change and pollution. Any transexodus turns our green visions grey. There is no choice to be made between transcendence and the concrete, between the other and the world; in the face of nothing we either have both or we lose everything.

Staying together

It is tempting to go one step further, not only back from Virilio to Wahl, but also from here forwards to the work of Emmanuel Levinas to add a robustly moral dimension to the above account of existence and exodus. For Levinas (2008b: 3, emphasis in original), transcendence is a 'passing over to being's *other*' or the 'otherwise than being'. As we have seen, this passing over is enacted in the encounter with the other person, who 'remains infinitely transcendent' and whose face calls me to a response and to responsibility (Levinas, 2007: 194). This account of moral experience encompasses Wahl's transascendence and transdescendence, as the other calls to me from 'a dimension of height, a dimension of transcendence', from beyond, 'committing me to human fraternity', but with a frail authority, from 'an essential destitution' that grounds the encounter in material acts of care and giving (Levinas, 2007: 215). Taken in this direction, we might say that rather than an exodus from earth, what we need instead is a stronger relationship with transcendence, a greater attention to the other here on earth, if we are to approach the coming catastrophe in such a way that avoids environmental injustice. There cannot be a revolution in morality without a radicalization of responsibility. We have found something radical like this in Levinas (see also Hill, 2019a), an account of moral experience that is not only grounded in confrontation with the infinite but also that asks infinitely of us, that would force us to go beyond what amounts to the good in the eyes of social institutions – and certainly beyond the reactionary vision of a green exodus that wraps its conservatism in science fiction. But it might not be enough.

Levinas's account of ethics as first philosophy is unavoidably humanistic, when what we seem to need is something altogether more expansive. Donna Haraway (2016) has argued that we are better off staying with the trouble to find solutions that work not only for all humans, but non-human animals and plants as well. Katharina Hoppe (2020) extends this into a call for a post-anthropocentric being with others, reclaiming a world of difference and dwelling together – or what she calls 'composing with otherness'. This may need to go yet further, to encompass what Kathryn Yusoff (2018b: 255) calls our 'mineralogical corporeality' – the way that we are, and that we always were, subjects of geology – in order to open our understanding of existence to our being with geological entities. We would find more to resist in the exodus to Mars, and more to gain here on earth, with an account of moral experience that recognizes our being towards animals and plants and minerals – a kind of *everyone and everything* responsibility. Such an account might yet be found with Levinas, although it is hoped that there is enough here through Virilio, and via Wahl, to make the case for existence against exodus.

A commitment to the ideology of growth and development that underpins the idea of *green exodus* transforms environmental catastrophe into a risk management exercise that is blind to diverse and unequal experiences of the existential crisis unfolding on the planet. The pursuit of speed and its disorientation of perception renders any such plan of escape a *grey exodus* in so far as it relocates the human to an environment alien to experience. In both its planning and its achievement, such a dislocation would be a divorce from transcendence, or a *transexodus*, that is unsustainable insofar as it disavows the relation with the other.

Musk and Bezos arm us with visions of taking off into space, hurtling upwards with the speed of progress, eyes locked on a green future away from the calloused and polluted planet that used to be home. Virilio gives us a very different image of the human transplant into space, the cosmonaut perforating the atmosphere at a speed that tears them from every known, staring ahead at an expanse of nothing, a desert future they are propelled towards with little hope of disembarkation, 'only the spectator of this perforation where the real is turned inside out like a glove' (Virilio, 2008a: 104). And Wahl (2017: 106) offers an alternative, to 'choose the world of problems, ruptures, and failures', with a 'gaze fixed toward a transcendence' that allows the individual to 'remain full of irreducible multiplicities and ruptures' and so to feel more intensely their own existence and its relation with the other. We can choose to reject the separation of transcendence and the concrete, to embrace a relationship with the transcendent and give up on exodus altogether.

Virilio (2007: 92–3) argues that to privilege space travel over dwelling on earth is an act of panic, an exodus to an uninhabitable exotic. The alternative lies in a renewed effort to *be with* – to *be for* – others here on earth, to find the transcendent in the concrete. To be clear, this is not an argument against all technological intervention. As Buck (2019) points out, embracing the world and intervening in it technologically are not mutually exclusive; the very worst that can happen is not that we turn to the tech billionaires but that we let them run riot and fuck it up. The litmus test, she says, is simple: Does the intervention advocated give us a liveable environment still 200 years into the future? As far as Mars is concerned, it does not provide a moral environment that is sustainable for any duration. We need to be less adventurous and more daring. This means recognizing that we are all bound up in this problem together, if only because what makes life worth living – living well together – involves us all in the first place.

It means, then, a radical reaffirmation of the moral gravity of our environment, a reorientation towards the other, and a renewed commitment to the inseparability of our ecological bodies – animal, terrestrial and social.

Interruption

We interrupt ourselves now to ask whether Emmanuel Levinas can really motivate us to stay together here on earth if he cannot motivate our responsibility towards non-human entities.

'From beginning to end', writes Richard Cohen (in Levinas, 2006c: xxvi), 'Levinas's thought is a humanism of the other'. The question then is how this *of the other* qualifies humanism in such way that makes it more morally useful than a humanism traditionally conceived in narrow anthropocentric terms. We need to be able to talk about human experience and about morality from the human perspective without losing sight of the specificity and limitation of this vantage point. What we want is a humanism of the other that is open to non-human others (the human is responsible for human and non-human others) and that at the same time permits us to be undecided about non-humanisms of the other (the responsibility of the non-human for human and non-human others is indeterminate). This would preserve both the seriousness and the strangeness of the non-human. We can have this with Levinas – but not without a little more care.

'Humanism', Levinas (1997: 273) himself recognized, is 'a much-used, misused and ambiguous word'. He agreed with the anti-humanists that the idea that the human (as an individual being) is the aim of reality is absurd (Levinas, 2006c: 56–7) but found his corrective in the idea that it is the other who gives the human their proper dimension, a corrective he found completely at odds with the anti-humanism of, for example, Martin Heidegger. 'Humanism', writes Levinas (2008c: 128), 'has to be denounced only because it is not sufficiently human'. It is in the welcome given to the other that Levinas finds what is meaningful about being human, and not culture, to which morality stands apart (Levinas, 2006c: 36); in care for others and not the vanity of human rationality that he strikes the foundation of humanism (Levinas, 2006c: 45). Even care for the self, as a kind of individual privilege, is revealed to be inadequate to support a humanism in the face of the death and suffering of others; instead, we must recognize the fragility of the human in humanism, a humanism with the other human at its centre, to decentre the self, but as a vulnerability. Human sovereignty is then challenged, not in the form of an anti-humanism but by the figure of the other person. We find humanity not in sovereignty or command but in passivity; that is, in the ability to go against nature – sketched somewhat crudely by Levinas as a red-clawed survival of the fittest – and when, in a gesture of giving, we go instead towards the other without concern for one's own condition nor for the conditioning of society that directs concerns this way or that at the expense of others.

What kind of a response is passivity? Levinas (2006c: 63) writes: 'The Ego from top to toe and to the very marrow is – vulnerability.' In encountering the suffering of the other, we are not only confronted with the vulnerability of another entity, but also with our own – not as some imagined sympathy or moral transitivism but as a demand to make ourselves vulnerable in response. Responsibility for others is itself 'an extreme vulnerability' (Levinas, 2006c: 67); we are vulnerable to the other's vulnerability. This is the utmost passivity. It is to break with the natural imperative of self-preservation. It is to understand our being directed not towards its death but towards the death of the other. To be human is to care for the other *before oneself.* Humanity as passivity is, then, a kind of non-indifference to the other, an openness to outrage and to being wounded, an exposure to the possibility of wounding when coming to the aid of others, an orientation towards that possibility without holding back, whatever may come in return, 'a passivity more passive than all passivity' (Levinas, 2008b: 15). 'The most passive, unassumable, passivity, the subjectivity or the very subjection of the subject', Levinas (2008b: 55) says, 'is due to my being obsessed with responsibility for the oppressed who is other than myself'. Passivity, which is to say responsibility as care, is humility, to let go of one's life project or works, one's commencements and commandments, one's own adventures, and to open oneself to the other person. It is to allow oneself to be interrupted by the other. This is not an openness in the sense of being showing itself. Nor is it, in the Heideggerian sense, an opening of consciousness, to go beyond being – beyond the particular – into the openness to comprehend some object (see Levinas, 1996: 2–10). It is instead an overflowing of comprehension in the encounter with the other as a particular being – an encounter with a face.

Naked, the last decent nakedness, the face speaks of the vulnerability of the other, of its destitution (see Levinas, 2006c: 9–44). But the real nudity of this face is not in its absence of clothing but in its absence of form, its trace of otherness, the absence or elusiveness of the other. The face represents a kind of gravity that disturbs, a disturbance of me, of ipseity (selfness), as a trace of illeity (incomprehension of absolute otherness). The nudity of the face means it has no cultural content, or that it escapes culturation at any rate, that the humanity of the other is not derived from its human culture but from its vulnerability, from the precariousness of its existence. And yet despite this vulnerability the face opposes me. Levinas (2006a: 19) writes that 'violence consists in ignoring this opposition, ignoring the face of a being, avoiding the gaze'. Violence, then, is to deny a being its individuality. The face is naked and in this nakedness, this withdrawal from my attempts to clothe it, to give it my own meaning, it says "no". This grave "no" is the impossibility of killing this other, which is to say, the possibility of encountering this other in a moral way. The face is then a peaceful opposition or rejection of my powers over it – of my ability to read into it any more than this prohibitive "no", this impossibility of killing a singularity in all its alterity.

How do we encounter the other who says "no" without reducing them to our own "yes", which is to say, without reducing them to the same? We need to make contact but contact with a singularity and without taking possession. 'Contact is tenderness and responsibility', writes Levinas (2006a: 116). It is a sensibility beyond consciousness or intentionality, a primary mode of sensibility in the form of a caress. Through touch we enter proximity with the other, insofar as it is tender, that it is a caress. For Levinas (2008c: 79), it is the separation of two hands touching – that the other hand is with mine but not mine – that signifies our intersubjectivity. This caress is an expression of the other's sensitive being. This hand, naked and vulnerable – like a face. The skin is present as a barrier, but the proximity of the one skin against the other is an encounter that takes us as close to this otherness as our separateness allows, even if the other always takes a step back and escapes my grasp. We are in proximity where the other is not reduced to sense data, is not encountered as some datum given over to me in perception, but as a singular being that impresses me, impresses upon me. When I look at the other, say, I do not possess an image that might contain them: 'The visible caresses the eye. One sees and one hears like one touches' (Levinas 2006a: 118). All encounter is touching in this way. It brings together 'an insurmountable duality of beings' in 'a relationship with what always steps away' (Levinas, 2008d: 86).

Should the other not move towards me? Levinas (2008d: 137) writes that responsibility 'is without concern for reciprocity: I have to respond to and for the Other without occupying myself with the Other's responsibility in my regard'. As John Llewelyn (1991: 7) observes, ethics would become 'totalitarian violence' if priority was not given to hearing the call for help as a call to me but instead as a universal principle that binds my neighbour too. My passivity puts others before myself without concern for how they orient themselves to me. I have no control over the actions of the other, nor insight into their thinking. I can sacrifice my needs for others, but I cannot demand the others do likewise; as Levinas (2008b: 126) quips, as close as he comes to quipping: 'to say that the other has to sacrifice himself to the others would be to preach human sacrifice!' Responsibility is mine alone. Or at least, only an 'I' can assume such responsibility. To be the one who says "I" is to be already the one who says "here I am", before the others and who goes towards the other, assuming the responsibility that can only be taken on and never asked of others. We have then an idea of passivity and the undoing of self-regard that is nonetheless bound up with the urgency of my response first and foremost. This is an idea of moral responsibility, then, that is tied to the first person.

As such, it can only really speak of human responsibility. If we are to work with an account of how a world of others is experienced as a world of encounters that obligate, and to say that, in the first personal mode of experiencing the world this is only ever an obligation that rests on the shoulders of whomever is doing the experiencing, then we would be forced to pass over in silence the moral experience of animals, since we should not be so bold as to imagine we might understand how they experience the world. Straightforwardly, the question of animal responsibility could not be contained by any account of human being, such as we find in the existential phenomenology of Levinas.

If this was the extent of the problem – that we do not claim to know animal experience and so speak only of human responsibility – then it would not, in the end, be so problematic for a humanism of the other. We could say that the human is responsible for others and leave open the question of who or what those others are. And we can say this despite Levinas maintaining that only the human can tear itself from animal nature and concern for its own being, that only the human is capable of passivity, since this cannot be determined by the phenomenological method Levinas employs. The real problem is that he closes off the more expansive option – of encountering whatever comes along and finding there the gravity of its existence – by arguing that the other can only be a human other, and so the human can only be responsible for the other human.

Levinas (2006a: 55) writes that in the interruptive encounter the other would 'oppose himself to me beyond all measure, with the total uncoveredness and nakedness of his defenceless eyes, the straightforwardness, the absolute frankness of his gaze'. It is in this encounter with a gaze that in its sincerity and its vulnerability counters mine, that true exteriority is experienced. One looks, but the other looks back; my vision cannot encompass the other, whose thoughts escape mine; the force of my looking is met by the vulnerable opposition of my being regarded. The other is unthinkable because they look at me from a height, putting me in question, an infinite overflowing of my comprehension or knowledge. Levinas (2006a: 119) calls this 'excession' and argues that it is only possible to be exceeded in this way when in an encounter with something that is absolutely other to me, a transcendence that disrupts 'the continuity of the concrete' (Levinas, 1996: 27).

Levinas maintains that it is only the other person, the other as a human neighbour, that opposes me in this way, who is met as an absolutely other, fundamentally elusive being. 'Men are absolutely different from one another', Levinas (1996: 27) suggests; 'the concept of man is the only one that cannot be comprehended, since each man is absolutely different from the other'. This is not to say that they do not have similarities, but that one cannot reduce the other to the same. Only an 'I' takes on responsibility, we know this, but more, it is only to a being that says "I" to itself that responsibility is due, since only such a being is so strange that it cannot be contained in my thought. This uniqueness demands a kind of moral substitution that is non-reciprocal. For Levinas (2008b: 117), substitution means that I substitute myself for the others, not as an interchanging nor as an imposition of my identity, but as a movement of passivity, a gesture so passive that it cannot be reduced to an act. This is the gravity of the other, that I am pulled towards the other, to be otherwise than being, but not to pull away or pull back in turn. Gravity is a graveness but also a movement – and still further a substitution that cannot be demanded in reverse. It is at the same time the demand for my responsibility and the undoing of my self-regard. But animals, in Levinas's reckoning, are interchangeable whereas the human – unique and encountered from above me – is not; and so the moral substitution performed by responsibility can only encompass the human. Levinas (1996: 17) is explicit that the 'absolutely Other is the human Other'; that is, that this otherness that his whole edifice of responsibility hinges on is only found with the human, because other entities can be known or contained or in some way translated to the same.

What are we to make of this? Llewelyn (1991: 83, 50) observes that Levinas – like Kant or Heidegger – was preoccupied with 'safeguarding the dignity of man', that when Levinas writes about animals it is 'almost always' with 'the animality of man' in mind, and that it is therefore difficult to discern what Levinas makes of animals themselves. But this is no defence against refusing the face of another, of course, even if it can get him off the hook for a narrowed human focus, and so it is difficult not to conclude that Levinas has a serious problem with animals. Bob Plant goes as far as to state that, despite warning against the reduction of the other to the same, Levinas was guilty of precisely this in the case of animals, was 'blindly anthropocentric' (2011: 54) and 'arguably speciesist' (2019: 31). At the very least, he fails to take animals seriously in his account of the seriousness of existence.

It is the position here that we can have Levinas's humanism of the other as long as it is not a humanism only of the human other. One way of achieving this, suggested by David Boothroyd (2019), is to say that Levinas has simply limited himself to an account of human existence, that his is an ethics of human vulnerability as it is experienced by humans, and that this does not exclude responsibility for the non-human – even though it does not explicitly offer a place to it. To expand on this, we can observe that if we are only responsible for a being that is absolutely other, and this is the case because it is only some entity that says "I" to itself that is properly elusive in this sense, then it is beyond me to locate it – for human being or any other. We can encounter a trace of this as a resistance in the height of the other, but then all we really have is some claim to having been resisted. Given that the encounter is entered into from a first personal perspective, then it cannot hope to survey an absolute otherness: excess, yes, but absolutely? From what vantage point would such a measure have to be made? The encounter is all we have, and so it would then be a more generous and open existence that took the other where it found it. This would leave us with a humanism that puts responsibility at the heart of human existence (see Zaka, 2011), that puts the 'I' at the heart of the moral universe, but that makes no claims that the human part of this equation is the end of it.

There are passages where some hope might be present that Levinas will open his responsibility to non-human animals and even non-animal others. His humanism of the other explicitly places the human at the centre of the world: 'I am man holding up the universe', he writes, a universe 'full of things' (Levinas, 2006c: 57). There is the danger here of reinforcing the anthropocentrism of the humanist tradition, but, just as the undoing of self-regard places me nonetheless at the front of moral life, this holding up of the universe is really only a perspective, or the motivation of a responsibility that is understood in first personal terms. 'The word *I* means *here I am*', writes Levinas (2008b: 114, emphasis in original), 'answering for everything and everyone'. There is something hopeful to be read in these words, of a responsibility for everyone and everything, and it is the placement of the individual at the centre of the moral universe that reveals the urgency of a decentring through responsibility, by going over to the other, and that gives us an idea of moral existence that ought to include the more than human. We should want to hold onto this much more expansive idea of moral gravity while leaving behind the aversion to animals.

Matthew Calarco consistently argues that we can have this cake and eat it. He points out that 'although Levinas himself is for the most part unabashedly and dogmatically anthropocentric, the underlying logic of his thought permits no such anthropocentrism' (Calarco, 2008: 55). That is to say that Levinas ought to be committed to a kind of agnosticism about who or what makes moral demands in the encounter, not because it is good to do so – it is – but because his work permits of no *a priori* constraints or stipulations. By this reading, Levinas's diminution of the moral gravity of the animal – in his defence of the human against its animal nature – and the contortions then made as to what moves me morally, are shown to be mere 'idiosyncratic restrictions' (Calarco, 2010: 125). We could then have an idea of responsibility that speaks to the human experience of moral existence while also allowing for the encounter with non-human others. We could say that Levinas is not blindly anthropocentric in a pejorative sense; he is simply closing one eye to look more closely at the human. This avoids a negative anthropocentrism – and certainly the charge of speciesism – by leaving open all moral possibility to the animal. And by consequence (although not without extensive work) to the non-human non-animal too. Calarco (2010: 127) characterizes his position as 'with and against Levinas', which seems to be a good vantage point for the consideration of any theoretical contribution, and its desirability in this case will be demonstrated anon in the response to three questions: *Can an animal be responsible? Does an animal have a face? Can an animal speak?*

We need now to interrupt Levinas with the interruptive force of gravity that belongs to the animal.

THREE

Responsibility

As we take stock of the end of the world, its richest men, Elon Musk and Jeff Bezos, advance plans for an interplanetary future that would sidestep our climate change and extreme weather, our accelerating desertification and faltering extinction. In the face of this vision of living off-planet, in contemplation of the force and the violence by which it would take us away from the gravity that binds us one to the other, it is not sufficient to simply say we should stay where we are. The world we have created here is limited insofar as it has been imagined insufficiently grave. What is needed now is a fuller account of the earth's gravity, of the pull not only of other humans but also of other lives here on this planet too.

In his essay on Martin Heidegger and Yuri Gagarin, Emmanuel Levinas (1997: 231) rejects the faith 'placed in the facilities that machines and the new sources of energy offer the childish instinct for speed' and that attaches to 'the pretty mechanical toys that entice the perpetually puerile adult'. But Levinas also rejects a Heideggerian critique of technology – that it represents the loss of identity as well as the exploitation of nature – because it is not hopeful enough. What hope when technological development 'risks blowing up the planet' (Levinas, 1997: 231) or driving us off its surface? For Levinas, a critique of technology must be founded on faith that the encounter with the other will lead to the discovery of our care for the other. We would then put our hope not in colonies on Mars or other off-world subsistence fantasies, not in the figure of Gagarin, blasted into 'the absolute of homogenous space' (Levinas, 1997: 233), but in the encounters of our moral existence. Levinas (1997: 22–3) would show us that the choice is not to trade the desert of a climate changed for the desert of space, but to find our lushness in others, and that we begin already in a desert that becomes habitable only in the response to the other being. We are exiled not to space but on earth, where we find meaning in sociality and in encounter.

But we cannot stay together alone as a species. We choose a human present or a future consummated with non-human animals. We must first come to terms with Levinas's humanism and go beyond his restriction of moral seriousness to the human being. Our reward would be the opening of the moral universe to the non-human animal, the grounding of our relationship with animals in a relation of responsibility, and a future that is morally sustainable. Jacques Derrida (2008: 12) worries that Levinas's humanism is 'a matter for serious concern' insofar as it excludes animals from our moral responsibility, but the corrective can be achieved within the spirit of Levinas's own work. Levinas's humanism underpins a moral relation without relation so radical that it needs must break with its own human chauvinism. The task is to extend the thought of Levinas beyond limitations he imposed but that appear as artificial barriers to the fullest goodness of its works. We would then occupy a position both with and against Levinas, deepening our attentiveness to moral gravity, further enriching what we have here on this planet, in this world we share with human others and animal others – and ultimately other others too.

And then the attraction of staying here, with all the others, would be felt greater still.

Animal response

So: *Can an animal be responsible?* For this to be the case in the sense given to responsibility by Levinas is difficult. I might be exposed in my encounter with the animal to a responsibility for its suffering – although this remains to be cashed out – but by what means can we understand this to occur in the reverse? Levinas (2008b: 47) writes that 'exposure to another ... is responsibility for the free initiatives of the other'. We might be tempted then to say that the animal cannot take responsibility for the free initiatives of another because it cannot comprehend the motivations or consequences of those free initiatives. And if the animal cannot be exposed to responsibility as a *going over to* the other then it exists in a state of solitariness. This is compounded by Levinas (2007: 149) describing such solitariness as 'animal complacency in oneself', one of the more explicit examples of the tendency to raise the animal predominantly in reference to the animality of the human. For Levinas, the human goes beyond the state of nature in its approach to the exterior and by the transformation of enjoyment of the other into responsibility for the other or living for the other. As such, the human, in Levinas's way of thinking, is above the natural order of things precisely because it rises above the animal condition.

In his famous 'Animal Interview', one of the rare occasions where he discusses animals as animals, Levinas (2019: 5) argues that the human is a break from pure being, that there is more to the human than just existence, and that this is because the human can identify something more important than its own life: that of the other. The implication is that animals are simply being. They exist for themselves and are incapable of existing otherwise than being, which is to say that they cannot exist for the other. The human, on the other hand, can recognize that being for itself is a kind of egoistic power, that power 'is by essence murderous of the other', and that responsibility is the transformation of power into the impossibility of murder in the encounter with the other (Levinas, 2007: 47). We might ask here why the power differential between human and animal does not appear to be murderous by essence, given that humans quite literally take possession of animals, and the answer would be that the 'thou shall not kill' does not emanate from the non-human – an answer to be rejected in due course – and that the human other is the only entity that the human can murder, since it is the only one that rises above the state of nature.

The other famous exploration of animals as animals by Levinas comes in the essay 'The Name of the Dog' where he recalls his encounter with a canine named Bobby. Here Levinas relates his time as Jewish prisoner of war held captive by the Nazis and his interactions with a stray dog that appeared to him to treat the prisoners with respect to their humanity, something denied to them by the guards. Levinas (1997: 152, emphasis in original) writes: 'At this supreme hour of his institution, with neither ethics *nor logos*, the dog will attest to the dignity of its person. This is what the friend of man means. There is a transcendence in the animal.' There is encouragement for those who want to extend responsibility to the animal in the idea that the animal has transcendence, but Levinas is clear: the dog is not an ethical animal, nor does it have the reason to be so. At best we can say from this story that the dog recognizes that Levinas and his fellow captives are capable of responsibility – perhaps towards the dog – because it recognized their humanity. For example: 'He would appear at morning assembly and was waiting for us as we returned, jumping up and down and barking in delight. For him, there was no doubt that we were men' (Levinas, 1997: 153). Levinas seems to be suggesting that the dog encountered the men as beings capable of looking after him but not that the dog was capable of being responsible for them in turn.

And then he does something odd: 'The dog was the last Kantian in Nazi Germany, without the brain needed to universalise maxims and drives' (Levinas, 1997: 153). This is unusual in two ways: first because Levinasian responsibility does not hinge on maxims being universalizable; and second, because Levinas cannot commit himself to an idea of moral encounter that is determined by rationality or comprehension. This is where the Calarco reading comes in. The exclusion of the animal on these grounds is not consistent with the account of responsibility that the animal is excluded from.

And Levinas knows this. In *Otherwise than Being* he writes that 'my responsibility for the other commands me before any decision, any deliberation' (Levinas, 2008b: 166). Rationality is neither here nor there when it comes to responsibility. Reason thematizes the one and the other in a system, whereas responsibility is anarchic, it is before any reasoning and resists reason's totalizing project. Responsibility is ultimately unreasonable.

Bob Plant (2011) pushes this point, recognizing that, for Levinas, moral responsibility goes against nature because it is an overcoming of our murderous will, that nature by this conception is a violent war of being, and that, as we know, there is an animality to this that is to be overcome through responsibility. But he also picks out, as above, the clear implication of Levinas's work that putting the other before oneself is not a rational or reasonable act. Nature is not overcome by some unique human cognitive facility. For Plant, this means that Levinas cannot deny responsibility to animals on the basis of their being incapable of rationality or reason. Animals, he concludes, may be stupid or they may not, but it makes no difference; moral good happens without it being reasoned into existence – or at least before. David Wood (2012) suggests that Levinas only excludes the animal from moral concern because he is preoccupied with overcoming human animality understood in this sense of murderousness. The logic here would be that: murderousness is something that is only present if it is possible to push against it and go instead peacefully towards the other; the human is capable of stepping outside the violent state of nature as a war of being and so of disavowing its murderousness; but the animal is not murderous because it is stuck in this war as mere being and so is unable to disavow murderousness. This would mean that the animal is incapable of giving, in its fullest sense, as a tearing away from preoccupation with its own struggle for existence. Calarco (2008: 55–77) suggests that, for Levinas, this inability to give moral responses then excludes the animal from receiving them – a reading also arrived upon by Llewelyn (1991: 53). But this again relies, at bottom, on the idea that the animal is not capable of moral reason, this time because it cannot choose not to do what it cannot do.

It is tempting to object to Levinas that the animal is quite capable of the things he denies to them. We might point here to the problem-solving of magpies or the care of a cat. On the latter point, we might say, with Jacques Derrida (2008: 14), that Levinas carries on like he has never even been looked at by an animal. But arguments as to what animals are and are not capable of feed a logic that ought to be resisted. An expansive responsibility that decentres the gravity of morality is desirable over and above the means testing of moral seriousness. There should be no appeal to reason to say that humans are morally different to animals, since it is the relationship to the other, and not reason, that makes humans human. As Atterton (2012) says, reason is a monologue; it is not for the other. It is when humans break with reason, and put the other first, that they are responsible. If we really need to decide whether animals are themselves responsible, then cognitive abilities are beside the point 'because the face to face as such does not involve the exercise of judgement-employing concepts' (Atterton, 2019: 71). The animal does not have to grasp anything to be responsible for others, since the encounter with the other is an encounter with the otherness of the other – an experience of ungraspability. As Michael Morgan (2019) argues, the question of whether animals are capable of moral responsibility is not going to be settled by scientific means – since such means were not in play to cash out human responsibility – but by how we are in the world with animals and they with us. If we then question Levinas's characterization of the state of nature and speak of how we are with animals in ways that at least suggest we have been looked at by them once in a while, then we can avoid the unpleasantness of cognitive barriers to moral status. For example, Judith Butler (2016: 46) argues that it is not a self-preserving drive that sustains life on earth but our interdependency. An account of moral responsibility grounded on vulnerability and suffering, as it is for Levinas, but that understood nature not as a war of being but instead as a community of beings, is, at the very least, more capable of responding to our catastrophic times.

For Boothroyd, the story of Bobby the dog is not so much about morality as it is enjoyment, in the specific sense given to it by Levinas, a state of being with the other in ways that are not themselves moral, since they nurture the self, since we enjoy and enjoy being enjoyed, but that open on to morality, that take us, at the very least, in that direction. Derrida (1999: 41) tells us, in his elegiac account of what matters most in the work of Levinas, how love of the other, as romantic love, as a requited enjoyment of the other, is not in itself moral, but that it is ultimately bound up in a moral life, since it directs me towards the other. We might say then that loving a cat or a bird or a stick insect might direct one towards the other, decentre one's concern, and play its part in living responsibly, so long as we did not limit this only to that cat or that bird or that stick insect. This would mean, as Boothroyd (2019: 772, emphasis in original) explains, 'that the animal would be said to find a place *in the overall picture* of Levinas' ethics'. We could then be bolder and say that the animal in turn enjoys the human, that we enter reciprocal relations of love, and say again that this opens onto morality, even if we must stop short of saying with any certainty that the stick insect is capable of moral responsibility.

This is a beginning, but it cannot be an end. As the end of the world approaches it would be the end of us all if this overall picture were not more robustly a moral community grounded in vulnerability and the abhorrence of our useless suffering. There is more work to do. But on the question of whether animals can respond morally, the answer should be that it does not matter. How would we know? Maybe it would be possible to feel the animal's responsibility to me in its response to me, but it would always be uncertain. I would always be left to wonder. Responsibility is in any event asymmetric and if we are to come to terms with the Anthropocene then that ought to dictate what direction responsibility goes in. That is, it seems more pressing at this juncture, defined by deleterious human adventure, for the human to give to the animal. It does not matter whether the animal is smart enough to give to me and it does not matter whether I get anything at all. The weight of responsibility is on human shoulders.

Facing animals

But: *Does an animal have a face?* If it does not, then we are left with *places in overall pictures* and not the much more demanding kind of moral encounter that is enacted in the face to face. Levinas (1996: 9) appears to box off this latter, more expansive – or more moving – kind of relationship when, in his essay 'Is Ontology Fundamental?', he compares the killing of a human with the killing of an animal or the felling of a tree, and concludes that the difference in these acts is that the first is the refusal of an encounter – to ignore a face – whereas the tree or the animal is not encountered with the same kind of gravity. This is where Derrida's chastisement about not being looked at comes in. A moral relationship is subtended by an encounter in which the other opposes me, not in aggression but by their singularity, their unassimilable and incomprehensible being. There is something elusive about the way the other looks at me, something that is not mine, something that is with the other – how they regard me – and that I am granted no access to. Another way of asking whether an animal has a face is to ask whether there is something closed to me with the animal, something that can only be encountered as a trace or a gesture. For Derrida (2008: 11) the answer is yes, that the animal 'has its point of view regarding me', which he calls 'the point of view of the absolute other'. By his reading, Levinas has limited the face to the human (even though it is not bound up in the flesh and blood of the human visage) so that the animal must therefore remain 'outside of the ethical circuit' (Derrida, 2008: 106). Derrida (2008: 107) finds this surprising, given that responsibility for Levinas is for the other and the other's infinite alterity, and that the animal is 'more infinitely other still, more radically other'.

It is tempting to go along with Derrida here, since, as he suggests, there is something in the encounter with the animal that, intuitively, can be read as a kind of vital aloofness; not an unfriendliness, or not in all cases, but a sense that the animal is not in my site, is a step away from me, or a step beyond. But this is not an argument that can be carried by appeal to degrees of otherness. Difference might be the subject of measure, where some entities are more different or more similar than others, but otherness is the non-comparability of one entity to another. Derrida cannot have it both ways: the animal cannot be absolutely other to me but also somehow more other to me than another human is; we should want to say instead that both the animal and the other human are absolutely other. Calarco (2019: 126) clocks this and points out that this otherness is come upon in the encounter not just with something that is exterior to me, but something that has an interiority that is never accessible to me. The face is the trace of this closed interior; it is, in Llewelyn's terms, 'the other's nonphenomenal singularity' (2003: 63). Non-phenomenal singularities are not the types of entity that bear comparison since they're not the kind of thing that can be measured or even fixed; the face is non-phrenological as well as being non-phenomenological – *because* it is non-phenomenological.

It is by rejecting Derrida's claim to the *more other than others* status of the animal that we can open a door that Levinas wants us to keep closed. As Llewelyn (1991: 250) points out, the face to face is a vertical dimension of height; it is not horizontal and so cannot be reduced to a relation between similar entities. The face to face exceeds or comes before any such classification. If naked need – as found in the nudity of the face – is what I respond to then the characteristics of that entity (including human / non-human) should not make any difference. Llewelyn (1991: 255) concludes that 'the naked alterity of a finite vulnerable thing suffices to put me under a direct responsibility toward it' and that 'qualitative similarity is not required'. As far as the need to respond goes, it should not matter what one responds to, only that a response is needed in the face of suffering or vulnerability. One nudity is as nude as any other in this regard; we should not find ourselves surprised or embarrassed if we find ourselves moved by the stick insect. Levinas recognized, of course, that there could not be a biological rationale for favouring the human over the animal; the other, after all, 'doesn't belong to a genus' (2006b: 177). So how does he do it? Calarco (2010) suggests that when Levinas says *human* he is picking out a moral entity rather than a species, one that has this particular moral gravity because it is capable of disrupting my egoism. As we will see shortly, this is going to get Levinas into a bit of trouble. But he is, in *Totality and Infinity* (2007: 73), adamant: 'it is only man who could be absolutely foreign to me – refractory to every typology, to every genus, to every characterology, to every classification'. The other human is separate to me and naked, but the animal can be captured and clothed by human activity.

Levinas is more circumspect in the (later) 'Animal Interview'. Here he declares: 'One cannot entirely refuse a dog the face' (Levinas 2019: 3), although this *entirely* is doing some confusing work. For Levinas (2019: 3), we might encounter the dog by its face, but the dog does not present a face 'in its purity'. In the dog Levinas (2019: 4) sees a 'force of nature' or a 'pure vitality', and it is these characteristics that reveal the dog before its face. But Levinas is also in this interview candid that he does not know at what point we can say that something has a face. He says that he does not know if a snake, for example, has a face, although he seems to rule out insects: 'Not in the flea, for example', he offers, when working through his uncertainty about what has a face; 'The flea! It's an insect, which jumps, eh?' (Levinas, 2019: 4). Ultimately, though, this ambiguity, with its arbitrary exclusions, is working to privilege the human. 'The wisdom of the face', Levinas (2019: 3) surmises, returning to more familiar – perhaps more obviously social – beings, 'does not begin with the dog'. We might (or might not) discover that an animal has a face, he says, but only after finding the human face, only as a rediscovery of the human face. Our sociality with animals would then have a moral dimension, but it is one that is secondary to, and participates in, human moral responsibility.

From this it appears that Levinas is uncertain about what has a face but persistent in his efforts to privilege the human encounter. Llewelyn (1991: 66) suggests that even though Levinas claims not to know if a snake has a face, even if it did, Levinas would maintain that it would not be in the same way that the human does. The snake's vulnerability, we might say, should we want to continue this line of thought, is less grave since it is not otherwise capable of going beyond its own existence, but this path has already been muddied above. The first part of Levinas's position, the uncertainty, might however be more fruitful. Calarco (2019: 128) argues that not knowing is not only consistent with Levinas's thought but also desirable for an animal ethics. That is, we can have no confidence when it comes to moral encounter and so should have no certainty about what will be encountered morally. An admission of non-knowledge is a moral position insofar as it is more hospitable than deciding in advance which entities are extended my care. Christian Diehm (2003: 172) extends a similar generosity in suggesting 'Levinas waivers on the question of others who are other-than-human because he remembers well his own philosophical principles', chiefly that the face cannot be thematized or comprehended and so the question of what has a face cannot be fixed.

With that door ajar, Plant (2011: 58) suggests we simply barge straight through it. We have to be uncertain about this, he says, because the encounter with a face will be specific to the encounter with a particular animal in its individuality. If we think at the level of genus – which Levinas cannot allow himself to do – then perhaps it does seem unusual to say that the snake or the flea or the clam has a face; but for the specific snake, this flea, that clam, we will have to see. Plant (2011: 60) suggests this is a 'charitable reading', but it is the only game in town. More than this, it is consistent with a responsibility for animals that deals not in masses but with individuals, not with abstractions but with encounters, which is necessary given the 'quick, quick, slow' nature of extinctions (Collard, 2018), since the individual loss is an urgent event of attrition that constitutes the ultimate but not sudden loss of species. We lose this sea turtle before we lose all sea turtles. Above all, to discuss the snake as a species is to beg the question; the face interrupts, and so to write off the moral gravity of an animal by its genus is to exclude in advance the possibility of it interrupting in order to exclude it in the end from moral consideration. Let the snake be on its own terms and all we can conclude is that it may or may not be encountered as a face when such an encounter occurs. As Boothroyd (2019: 773) explains, not only can we not know what has a face, but also we cannot even know, ultimately, who or what faces us. The face is an enigma.

If we cannot say in advance that a given animal has a face, what would, in the event, rule it out? It would have to be that in the encounter, we have – possess and not merely feel that we have – the measure of the beast. We can study the animal of course, and in this way Levinas says that science would clothe it, disclose it – or even give it form. But he is also alive to the violent exclusion of the unreasonable by a state that wraps itself in the rational discourse of science (see Levinas, 2008b: 170), so it is an unfamiliar tool to wield in the context of the animal. It is very much not in the spirit of Levinas's writing that science might know all there is to know of the animal, that nothing escapes it, such that the individual critter is a closed case.

An alternative means of maintaining his animal exclusion is to hold that the animal is enjoyed and that in this way is taken possession of. Levinas explains possession in 'Is Ontology Fundamental?' (1996: 9) as follows: 'It is not only a question of the fact that the being is an instrument, a tool, that is to say, a means. It is an end also. As consumable, it is nourishment, and in enjoyment, it offers itself, gives itself, belongs to me.' As Alphonso Lingis (2019: 22–3) points out, other animals would be, for Levinas, phenomena that exist as entities for me, and as such would have no otherness and present no face. While the other human resists me, cannot be assimilated to my projects or ambitions, the animal's resistance can be overcome.

It is tempting to observe that this is not always the case. If Levinas had not been looked at by an animal, as Derrida suggested, then we could go further and say perhaps he had never been half-eaten by one either. Calarco (2015: 59–61) gestures at this when he evokes Val Plumwood's (1995) philosophical account of becoming prey to a saltwater crocodile. Perhaps only the human can contain the animal in thought, but some of them, can, of course, contain us elsewhere. This is somewhat extreme, but we can also point to the experience of being looked at as prey – stalked by the bear or circled by the shark.

In the final reckoning, however, this is no good. The other does not resist me with its violence but with its pacifism. In the encounter with the face, I am moved not by its gesture of predation but by its expression of vulnerability. The face, as Butler (2006: xviii) presents it, communicates what is precarious and injurable. There is no vantage point from which to say that no aspect of the animal has escaped me – because it would have escaped me. From within this limitation, we do not need to imagine being prey but to accept what we cannot imagine. And what we cannot imagine is the suffering of the other, the way that its useless suffering truncates its ability to be in the world. I am not surpassed by the animal because it can eat me; I am decentred by the animal because it is vulnerable. As Calarco (2010) observes, for an animal to have a face it would simply need to be capable of expressing a vulnerability that calls my ego into question. Is this such a high bar?

Animal saying

Or: *Can an animal speak?* We know that for Levinas we encounter the other through touch − not as a sensorial enjoyment but as proximity to what remains separate. But for Levinas, while this motivates responsibility in touching humans, and spreads tenderness, the animal is calloused by the caress. 'In stroking an animal', Levinas (2006a: 118–19) claims, 'already the hide hardens the skin'. These remarks are made in the essay 'Language and Proximity', which gives a much fuller account of the seriousness of saying than it does of touch. Here we see Levinas's sympathy towards a Cartesian account of animals: that they cannot speak to humans and so cannot speak to each other.

The moral importance of saying is developed also in 'Is Ontology Fundamental?' and finds its fullest expression in *Otherwise than Being*, where it takes on a greater urgency than even the tenderest of caresses. In the former, Levinas argues that the encounter is so much more than comprehension of the other; in the encounter I speak to the other, encountering the other as a particular being, and in so doing I communicate this encounter in turn to the other. 'A human being', says Levinas (1996: 7), building on this odd Cartesianism, 'is the sole being which I am unable to encounter without expressing this very encounter to him'. Such an encounter with a human other is then, as such, always a greeting: we encounter as we speak and we speak the encounter. This is not to say that such a communication of the encounter to the other deposits the thought of it into their mind; this communication of sociality is 'irreducible to comprehension' (Levinas, 1996: 7). Like touching, this communication approaches only so far until it encounters the separation of the other's interiority from mine; it is an encounter with an exterior that nevertheless rises above animal encounter since what it communicates is that there is a moral encounter – something Levinas holds an animal could not communicate. We reach here the now familiar problem (for maintaining the Levinas line) that the animal cannot be excluded on grounds of being unaware that such an encounter is being undertaken, since comprehension is beside the point. The exclusion would have to be on the basis, already bought in from Descartes, that the animal cannot speak. In order to see why the animal might be considered speechless, we first need to approach what moral function speech performs.

In *Totality and Infinity* Levinas (2007: 195) writes that 'speech cuts across vision', which is to say that it interrupts the imperial tendency of sight to take in the other, to essay the other and thereby assail their singularity. Speech's cutting across makes it impossible to contain things in vision, or to thematize them by replacing those things with signs; it is an interruption of my being by the being of the other showing itself. Speech is fundamentally jarring, in that morally useful way of reminding the one of the elusiveness of the other. We cannot sublate our ears and evade the encounter with an entity who pierces our hypostasis with their saying. Levinas (2007: 195) explains that 'the ethical relationship which subtends discourse is not a species of consciousness whose ray emanates from the I; it puts the I in question. This putting in question emanates from the other.' This saying of the other is morally serious insofar as it unsettles and decentres the self. Like touch, it is a contact with singularity, but one that is perhaps more explosive in making itself felt, since the other touched resists me whereas the other's speech pierces my solitude and puts me into question.

To get to grips with the supposed speechlessness of the animal we also need to be clear on what speech is not. In *Otherwise than Being* Levinas writes that 'responsibility for another is precisely a saying prior to anything said'. This distinction, between saying and the said, that we have seen before in Blanchot and in Levinas, not only sets apart the interruptive from the regurgitative, it also makes plain that saying cannot be reduced to the content of speech. Saying would then be, more precisely, a movement beyond essence, and does not map on exactly to utterances or acts. As such, speech does not need to make sense to be morally moving, indeed, might even lose something the more intelligible we find it. 'Words are symptoms or superstructures', Levinas (1997: 206) writes, in the playfully titled essay 'Freedom of Speech', 'such that conscious cries and gestures form part of the nightmare they tried to interrupt'. He goes on: 'By being coherent, speech has lost its speech' (Levinas, 1997: 207). This might appear to give hope that howls and croaks and hisses might come to bear morally on human ears, but Levinas appears to leave no room for such a reading. This is because, by his reckoning, speech requires interiority. Saying is 'a being telling itself to us independently of every position we would have taken in its regard' (Levinas, 2007: 65); it is a saying expressed not in the light of me or how I would announce it, nor as a disclosure to me, nor even as a form, but as a formlessness, as a face. It is in this sense that Levinas believes that animals talk neither to humans nor to each other: they do not present a face that interrupts. Having ruled out the possibility of the animal being responsible or having a face, Levinas (2006a: 124) squares the circle: responsibility 'is the source of speaking' and it is this language that makes us human. We are human because we speak and we only speak insofar as we are beings capable of going beyond nature and taking responsibility for the other. Llewelyn (1991: 58) concludes that, according to the Levinasian account of moral responsibility, we are responsible only towards beings that can speak – and so the animal is contained in the said and left ultimately mute.

What does this mean for Boothroyd's position that the story of Bobby the dog is one of enjoyment and that, by extension, the relation to the animal opens onto moral experience even if it is not itself a moral encounter? Levinas (2007: 76) argues that separation allows for enjoyment and possession, that it is the constitution of thought and interiority, and that this being at home with oneself is disrupted by the saying of the other, which demands that possession becomes instead giving. If we can say that an animal can speak, with and against Levinas, then we can avoid relegating them to possessions of enjoyment in the first place. In defence of Boothroyd's reading we can point to Llewelyn (1991: 121), who suggests that saying does not dispense with the said, just as the face does not escape the physical, and so otherness is bound up with sameness, and from here responsibility emanates; that is, that even enjoyment of things possessed can become responsibility. This would give us further licence to say that we cannot know *a priori* which speech cuts through morally and which does not, but Levinas's triangulation of human–speech–responsibility would still box us in. Plant (2011) argues that, for Levinas, it is the silence of animals, in the sense of their inability to form words, that picks out their moral inferiority to humans, but this risks placing too much importance on the sound of saying and not its gesture – although, it must be said, Plant is only responding to Levinas's own looseness here. Levinas dismisses the grunts and howls of animals as being morally unserious, and Plant is correct to point out that this is contradictory to Levinas's own formulation of the saying versus the said. Plant (2011: 60) asks, if the animal noise is inferior, then is the human cry of pain less vital than the words 'this hurts'? But the difficulty with this line of argument is that Levinas would simply say no, on the grounds that the cry of pain emanated from the human.

Llewelyn (1991: 194) takes a similar line to Plant, asking whether the other can call me to responsibility if it cannot speak and answering: 'why not?' We can recognize that both animals and humans can have needs even if they cannot put them into words. As Diehm (2003: 178–83) argues, the question should not be *who speaks?* but *who suffers?* and the answer is that every body suffers; every body that has life struggles for its existence and bears on us morally, which is to say that every body has moral gravity. That I can go beyond struggle and towards the other is only an argument for me to hear the vulnerable other in whatever form it is encountered; whether it speaks or not itself with a human voice is beside the point. If the animal calls me to it, which is to say that I am moved by its precarity, then it has communicated to me that there is a moral encounter simply by being the source of this gravity. Levinas (2006a: 119, 123) wrote in 'Language and Proximity' that proximity is 'a language without words' and that it is this relationship – what he calls 'fraternity' – that makes us human. In which case, we can either attempt to gerrymander what counts as such a language or be open to the idea that lots of non-human entities might in any event turn out to be human or else get off the merry-go-round altogether and conclude that the best we can say is that suffering demands a response and that this is communicated in the encounter with something vulnerable.

Calarco chooses to expand what is meant by *human* so that we can maintain that animals are capable of speech in this moral sense. He argues that if the call of responsibility comes from outside – 'ultimately arising from heteronomous sources' – then there is no way of determining in advance where it will come from (Calarco, 2019: 123). It could feasibly be any entity to the extent that it communicates, in the encounter, that I ought to give up on mastery over what is outside the self and instead simply give. If we cannot restrict how we are called or predetermine how we will respond to this call, then why restrict who might call us? 'If ethics arises from an encounter with an Other who is fundamentally irreducible to and unanticipatable by my egoistic and cognitive machinations', asks Calarco (2010: 126), 'then how could this question ever be answered fully?' Calarco's agnosticism would mean that not only is it impossible to rule out what entities initiate moral encounters but also that, by extension, and given the definition that the human is an entity that is capable of disrupting my egoism, we would have to be agnostic about what entities are humans too. And if it appears absurd to say that a tree is morally moving or that a dog is a human, he concludes, then no matter; Levinas had already told us that responsibility is beyond reason.

Such a move is certainly appealing; if Levinas wants to operate with so loose a definition of what it means to be human then why not poke our fingers in and stretch it out a bit? The ascription of humanity to animals might feel profligate if ontological parsimony is desired, but the categorization of things is, in a Levinasian moral universe, much less important than responding to the encounter with the face and to the call, which is what drives this expansive ascription of humanity to begin with. It is a live option, but a curious one; do we want to live in a world of humans – even humans so varied as to be in fact dogs or pigeons or squids – when we want to be careful about the otherness of the otherwise than human?

Let us instead say that humanity is simply responsibility when it is given by the human and leave it at that. If the encounter with suffering arouses my goodness then we can call that my humanity, if we like, since it is mine, and I am human, and I make no claims as to how anyone else – human or animal – encounters the same thing, but it is a very narrow reference point, to say the least. More than this, it is perhaps the least interesting thing about such a moral encounter, the locus of which is the other and not the responsible individual. We can have a *human*ism of the other but also hold open the idea that there are other *isms* of the other – who knows? – and get down to the real business of tending to the oppressed and the wounded and the suffering. A humanism of the other would then, and finally, be a responsibility given to precarious others, precarious because other, who we need not call humans but to whose call we must heed.

The animal speaks in so far as it is vulnerable, which is a vulnerability to me, to my actions and my projects, to my adventures in the world; it speaks without words, with its suffering, saying what only the vulnerability of life can: *thou shall not kill.*

Suffering animals

The closest Levinas offers as a solution to the animal problem of his own doing is a kind of compromise that would maintain the human prejudice while recognizing the seriousness of animal suffering. He does this in the 'Animal Interview' (2019: 4) when he states that 'even if animals are not considered as human beings, the ethical extends to living beings. I really think so', suggesting that we humans do not want to cause needless suffering in animals, but that human ethics would have to be the 'prototype' for this kind of extended responsibility. Llewelyn (1991: 65), reflecting on these remarks, suggests that Levinas is indicating a distinction between obligation and responsibility, that we have certain obligations to animals but not responsibility in the fullest sense that we extend it to humans. This would mean that we might care for animals but only as a kind of facsimile of responsibility for humans, and one that is secondary to the prototypical human relationship. It must remain secondary, as Plant (2019) points out, because Levinas wants to retain the possibility that while the suffering of the human other is useless, the suffering of the animal might sometimes be necessary.

It is difficult to motivate much enthusiasm for such a distinction, given that there is no god's eye view that would allow us to disentangle the imperative of necessity from what appears useful from a human perspective. It is hard to see how it would not also be a kind of imperialism of the same. It also feels somewhat unambitious. At least Friedrich Nietzsche (2013) wanted to argue that the suffering of the other was useful to the other; here it would be useful only on human terms and which seem to offer nothing more novel than a kind of utilitarian chauvinism. It risks a circularity that is self-serving, presenting the animal as something that can be used up like a possession because we have no responsibility for it when we seem to have no responsibility for it because it is the kind of thing we tend to use up like a possession. It is precisely because the suffering of the other limits its possibilities of being that we are responsible and must give help; we should not limit those possibilities in advance by deciding upon what suffering matters and what is excusable or desirable.

In the end, Levinas is anthropocentric about responsibility but not humanist in a traditional sense (human subjectivity grounded in autonomy and agency). His humanism appears robust only in conjunction with that account of responsibility but is weak in isolation, and, as such, offers insufficient support to his exclusion of animals. Levinas's humanism picks out what is morally grave: those others that move me to respond; and the gravity of my responding. If we reject the enclosure that this humanism seeks to enact – since the animal calls me and presents a face and since its responsibility in my regard is neither here nor there – then we have, with and against Levinas, an account of moral responsibility that is enacted when precarious lives present themselves to our moral experience. This is an account of responsibility that would recognize that what matters is not to possess but to give to others. Animals are then not there for me only to enjoy; when they are there, on my hands, in my site, in need of me in some way, then I am there for them. The animal weighs on me. I give to the animal as I do the human because despite everything their suffering is incommensurable – and because their suffering is.

This raises a final problem. When Levinas says that I am responsible for everything and everyone we can say that everyone might (who could know?) include the newt or the bee or the sprat. But everything? Responsibility for Levinas means recognizing also that things are not there for me to possess but to give to others. If this is the case, then even if we can elevate animals to the moral universe, we are not yet able to incorporate plants and rocks and other such non-animal entities, since they remain gifts rather than recipients.

Without them, we are not staying together but already on the run from responsibility. And our catastrophe has always been a flight from the world.

FOUR

Accession

A case has been made to take seriously the demands placed on us by non-human animals. This would allow for us to accommodate the experience of being called to responsibility in the encounter without situating a moral entity within a hierarchy that prioritizes the human *qua* human. This is not an account of moral responsibility that operates with any certainty; it is instead mobilized by its own uncertainty about what presents a face and how this encounter is experienced.

But is this enough? If the Anthropocene marks the impact of human activity on geological time, then it is time in turn to open our responsibility more generously to geological entities. As Matthew Calarco (2015: 36) points out, opening moral responsibility to animals before then extending this to the non-animal is a strategic move in a wider ecological ethics and, although he has in mind a longer form of social change, we know already, although the question is not settled – and should not be settled – that there are persuasive grounds to accept that the account of responsibility found in the work of Emmanuel Levinas ought to apply to animals also. The argument now is that if we are to find something worth saving in the Anthropocene, where the human lives oversized in the geological record, and if we are to find it here and resist the pull of Mars, or the push of entrepreneurs, then we must begin from our *being for geology*. Levinas (2006c: 56) wrote that 'nothing is more comical than the care for itself taken by a being doomed to destruction'. Well then, if we are to find hope and escape doom, we need to extend responsibility beyond the human and beyond the animal and towards the geologic.

Nigel Clark and Kathryn Yusoff (2017: 6) have called time to 'geologize the social', to acknowledge that among the many ways the 'I' is decentred is its deep coexistence with the geological, and that any critique of the social conditions that bring us to the point of catastrophe cannot exclude the way that we are bound up in a geologic life. As Clark (2013) makes plain, no account of what to do when the human becomes a geologic force is complete without an understanding of how geologic forces shape the human. Yusoff (2017) argues that just as there is no such thing as an apolitical account of the Anthropocene, it is also not possible to have a political critique without geology. In this spirit, if we are, as Levinas suggests, to find our hope in the morality of the encounter, then we need to work from an understanding of sociality that includes the geologic, and this in the sense of an openness to what Manuel Tironi (2019) identifies as the radical otherness of geological entities.

If extending responsibility to animals was not without difficulty then doing the same for, as David Boothroyd (2019: 771) terms it, 'nonhuman nonanimal alterity' poses its own problems. We are in pursuit of a moral ecology that would take seriously the moral demands of the environmental, not as facilitator of human being but as singular entities to be encountered, existences that must be negotiated. This would be something along the lines set out by John Llewelyn (2003: 58): 'A philosophical ecology deeper than one concerned only with the human being's environment would be one that follows up the consequences of the thought that as well as having an environment the human being is part of the environment of nonhuman beings.'

This is difficult in the case of geological entities and processes because of the way that they are received by the human imagination. The geological seems to form a broadly stable platform on which human activity is undertaken, while its own dynamism is hidden outside the eruptive qualities of volcanoes or the ground-shaking tendencies of earthquakes. Beyond the horror of this breaching, geological entities are not taken to be the kinds of things that impress themselves upon the human in encounter, such that while the rock face presents itself as a challenge to be conquered by human prowess, it is more difficult to motivate the idea that it presents a face in this moral sense, that would challenge our human egoism. The stone does not appear to have needs or even really an existence comparable to that of the human or the animal. Its time is not regarded as pressing.

We need to work through these difficulties in pursuit of an account that takes seriously our commitment to the geological, and more broadly to the non-human and non-animal. This endeavour is given hope by Edward Casey's (2003: 193) observation that Levinas ultimately realized his choice was to limit moral responsibility to the human or else extend it to everything and lose the special status afforded to human existence. And so Levinas's ethics is a *human ethics*. But it need not be so. The task now is to imagine instead an *everything ethics* with the geological as its motivator. Then we would have in mind a case for the accession of the geologic to the moral universe and an understanding of being for geology that accedes to the indifferent need of the rock, which is also our need, for this planet together, in wellness and well into the future.

Deep time

The human was always already geologic. Kathryn Yusoff (2015) argues that the geological is constitutive of our human identity, that geological time may be excessive or inhuman in its duration, but is, nonetheless, contributory to who we are now. This rests on an understanding of the non-human that allows for its great inheritance to human existence, that recognizes that it is not outside human experience or subjectivity.

Being human is of course different to being a rock; for Yusoff (2015: 401), it is not that we form a hybrid with stone, or a network or a meshwork, but that we are multiply authored by 'temporal and immaterial registers' that include the deep and often imperceptible processes of the geological. Yusoff (2013: 784) tethers the 'geoformation of subjectivity' to the capitalization of fossil fuels, and while this is one of the important stories to be told of the human being geologic, we want something more too. We can say, as does Yusoff, that combustion is part of what it means to be a subject in late capitalism with some confidence. And it is useful to do so, as it forces us to confront the twin impact of this relationship: on how the geological is there in human capitalist development; and how that human capitalist development is there deleteriously now in the geologic record. But there is also an opportunity to think of our 'mineralogical corporeality' or 'geologic agency' (Yusoff, 2018b: 255, 288) as motivations to a more expansive account of how our being is bound up with the non-human non-animal other – the *everything other* – through our co-constitution and its resultant responsibility through deep time.

In *Existence and Existents* (2008a) Levinas identifies the 'I' – the individual given to responsibility – with the present, arguing that they are, in fact, the same event. The 'I' is the presence of the present and not of duration (understood here in the sense of Henri Bergson as a heterogeneous flow of the past into the present and beyond) and needs the other to go into the future. Time, he wagers, must come from the other, since the 'I' is itself just one instance, and so the encounter of the one with the other reveals that sociality is time itself. These ideas are further developed in the roughly contemporaneous work *Time and the Other* (2008d). Here Levinas (2008d: 30, 32, emphasis in original) writes that time is 'the relationship of "thought" to the other'; that is, 'the relationship to *that* which – of itself unassimilable, absolutely other – would not allow itself to be assimilated by experience; or to *that* which – of itself infinite – would not allow itself to be comprehended'. Time then signifies that the 'I' and the other never coincide, that they are instances out of sync, but also it signifies the relationship of the 'I' and the other that is an 'awaiting' to be aspired to (Levinas, 2008d: 32). As such, time is a movement towards the infinity of the other; it is fundamentally social. Levinas (2008d: 39) argues that 'time is not the achievement of an isolated and lone subject'; it is instead 'the very relationship of the subject with the Other'. Only when we introduce (in some ontological sense) time can we go beyond our hypostasis – beyond this instance that is mine alone – and towards the other. Solitude is an absence of time. Responsibility is the future. Time is the shattering of hypostatic egoism. This account of the moral condition of the future is vital to any grounding of responsibility to those entities and processes that we habitually exclude, whether that is for their distance from our own humanity or the lack of liveliness in comparison to privileged animals. But it also opens up the question of our pessimism about the future – a future of quick, quick, slow extinctions and desertification and extreme weather and all other manner of climate catastrophe – and then situates it squarely within the purview of responsibility.

The unknowability of a future consummated with the other gives us hope only if it motivates a more expansive idea of the gravity of the world. Levinas (2008d: 77) writes: 'The other is the future. The very relationship with the other is the relationship with the future.' The future so understood is to enter a relationship with the present moment and the encounter that takes it forward in time. That is to say that the relationship between our present and the future is 'accomplished in the face-to-face with the Other. The situation of the face-to-face would be the very accomplishment of time; the encroachment of the present on the future is not the feat of the subject alone, but the intersubjective relationship' (Levinas, 2008d: 79). In this way, the future is understood as something new in the sense of being absolutely other to the present. Likewise, the other is inaccessible and so always still to come. Neither future nor other ever arrives or else they become the present and the same. I am then always moving towards something that recedes from my power. This furnishes us with an understanding of time, as Levinas (1997: 292) notes in his essay 'Signature', as 'a mode of existence in which everything is always revocable, in which nothing is definitive but everything is yet to come'. This is an understanding of time and our relationship to the future that welcomes the rupture, the rupture of speech or of responsibility, those crashing, eruptive, interruptive events of moral existence that simultaneously puncture and sustain moral experience. This is time as being tearing itself away from the totality of its present in the encounter with alterity. It is a useful conception since, as Llewelyn (2010: 108) observes, 'the pastness, presence, and futureness of the existence of something are relevant to whether and how it is a subject of ecoethical consideration'. This is important in the context of geological processes, where the urgency of environmental catastrophe must be thought in terms of a relationship that extends backwards through deep geological time in order to take us forwards into a future that is not hostile or barren or else withdrawn beyond reach.

Why deep time? It is possible to look through human history to the capitalization of carbon to understand our intimate moral relationship with the geologic. Likewise, we could look also to the way that human culture is bound up with geological entities. Irene Klaver (2003: 161), for example, indicates the way that stones 'are messages of other times, themselves painted and coded with messages, times of other civilisations, cultures long gone'. Similarly, Jeffrey Cohen (2015) gives us a rich account of the force of stone in the medieval mind (and much more besides). These are important stories. But they are human stories, and they tell us much more about the co-constitution of rocks and culture than they do about the moral seriousness of rocks in themselves. We must look to the stones and the magma unadorned by the human or else we risk limiting responsibility to what serves human culture or development.

One way of doing this is to recognize, as Clark and Gunaratnam (2017) indicate, that geology is a complex system that reorganizes itself, and that it does so at speed. While the former point is intuitive in thinking geologically without human prejudice, the latter is perhaps less so – precisely because it is in this way that the human is brought into confrontation with processes that exceed it. Clark and Gunaratnam highlight how human life is influenced by the movement of tectonic plates by magma and the stratal composition of the earth's crust. Vannini and Vannini (2020) argue that we think of these geological processes as something that happened millions of years ago, giving to us the world as we experience it now, but these are processes that are still occurring, all around us, under our feet, before our eyes. As Cohen (2015) points out, rock is always in motion, seismic and only apparently in stasis. Following these lines of thought through, then, requires an understanding of deep time that is attuned to geology's inhuman liveliness: the way that its changes are abrupt according to their own temporality. Earthquakes and volcanoes and these other eruptive moments are interruptive to human experience because they are manifestations – what Clark, Gormally and Tuffen (2018: 275) call 'breachings' – of deep time intervening in everyday human rhythms. These breachings do not just have an immediate or emerging impact; they have evolutionary significance. This is not to say that the eruptions of volcanoes or the seismic reorganization of earthquakes determine human existence or reality, but that the human is '*becoming with* volcanic and magmatic process' (Clark, Gormally and Tuffen, 2018: 289). If this is the case, if we are still now *becoming with* these geological processes, then the future opens before us together. Put another way, being for geology would be a movement towards a different world.

What we should want to say, then, thinking across Levinas and Clark and co, is that the human moment is a stuckness and that the possibility of this future rests not here but on the lively-slow movement of geology, its duration as deep time.

Privileging human time sustains its non-coincidence with geological time. To relinquish this privileged disposition before the world and embrace the unassimilable, to encounter the inhuman liveliness of geological processes, would remove us from the masquerade of the human present and take us towards a future with geological being that is appropriate to our deep past formed by geological becoming. The 'temporal alterity' (Cohen, 2015: 192) of geology is an opening on to community with the human, an invitation and not an impediment. Let not only the volcano be eruptive. Let glaciation and tectonic movement and the encounter with this rock, here and then forwards in time together, be recognized as the shattering of hypostasis. And then, this moment shattered and brought into duration, this individual – 'me' – and my narrow concern interrupted, we might talk of the yet to come, and perhaps even to hope, pessimistically.

Surface dwelling

Here we hit upon a problem. Levinas's account of time and the other appears, when that other is geological, to come up against his spatialization of responsibility. In *Totality and Infinity* Levinas (2007: 152–74) sets out his account of dwelling as the condition and commencement of moral activity. His figure of the dwelling is the home, although this represents more so the concretization of the separateness of the 'I' than the bricks and mortar of a given house. 'Concretely speaking', writes Levinas (2007: 153), 'the dwelling is not situated in the objective world, but the objective world is situated by relation to my dwelling'. The home then represents both an inwardness and an openness; it is in the world but is also my opening onto the world.

Straightaway we can say that the problem of Levinas's spatialization is not that the geological is merely the stuff of homes or habitat. In fact, the opposite would be the case. For Levinas, the home is the space of moral existence and yet it must as a result be distinct from the natural world. He writes: 'The home does not implant the separated being in a ground to leave it in vegetable communication with the elements. It is set back from the anonymity of the earth, the air, the light, the forest, the road, the sea, the river' (Levinas, 2007: 156). The home breaks with the elements and allows for the 'I' to recollect itself, to allow interiority for itself, so that it can then open the home to the other in the gesture of hospitality or responsibility. This interiority makes possible a relationship with its exterior. Dwelling is to be at home with oneself but not for oneself. It is to welcome or to give. 'I welcome the Other who presents himself in my home by opening my home to him', says Levinas (2007: 171).

The real problem is that, in defining the human as a being able to break with nature, Levinas is left with a spatial account of responsibility that breaks with the natural environment. If plants and rocks and all other manner of things are anonymous, then they cannot be welcomed. We cannot give to the faceless.

This is further complicated when we dig in deeper to Levinas's elements. Levinas (2007: 104–5), again in *Totality and Infinity*, makes plain his position that although the human is dependent on its environment to exist, it is from this relationship to the elemental that the human draws its exteriority to the totality or system of nature. The elemental here picks out those forces or processes that contain but cannot themselves be contained: the seas, the light, the earth. All possession is situated within these non-possessable environments. The elements are non-possessable because even though we can know the forces that shape them, we are irrevocably within them; there is no position from which, having stepped outside the elements, we can take them in in totality. While I cannot myself contain the whole sea, I might float on its surface; while I cannot possess the source of the element, I can be nourished by it. That said, even though we are in the elements, this is not sufficient, for Levinas (2007: 131), to claim that the elements represent an encounterable exteriority, because we are, nonetheless, at home in the elements. They may be indeterminate but that is not to say that they are infinite. To be at home with oneself is to enjoy the elemental, to live from the nourishment of the world. Levinas (2007: 110) says: 'We live from "good soup", air, light, spectacles, work, sleep, etc.' This strange mix is, apparently, united as objects of enjoyment. But our enjoyment is to transmute the other into the same, and while we *live from* this broad soup and its 'quenching' (Levinas, 2007: 113), we *live for* others. We do not encounter morally those things that nourish us; we give them to the other in the gesture of responsibility.

Can we take from the environment to give to the environment? Perhaps yes, in a utilitarian account, but if we want a humanism of the other that responds to the non-human other, then we cannot be sacrificing the one alterity to the other. Jacques Derrida recognized that all giving in a finite world ultimately ran into the problem of incalculability. 'How would you ever justify the fact that you sacrifice all the cats in the world to the cat that you feed at home every morning for years', asks Derrida (1995: 71), 'whereas other cats die of hunger at every instant? Not to mention other people?' But it probably warrants mentioning that rarely do we feed cats to cats, which is where we end up if we tether our account of geological giving to an understanding that the natural world is simply there for humans to take from. And although we do feed other animals to cats, we are looking now for an account of moral responsibility that operates without the hierarchies that make this permissible, because we are looking for an account of moral responsibility that recognizes the singular existence of non-human non-animal identities.

For Levinas, the elemental can have no face because I am in it; I never encounter its side, its visage, it does not conceal something that can be encountered; the element is an ever-renewed absence, an existence without an existent. As Levinas (2007: 149) frames it, our relationship with the material world is the 'enjoyment and agreeableness of life'. Agreeableness or enjoyment, as we know, are bound up with interiority. And even if we are tempted to say that often the world is, of course, disagreeable – and the concerns of this book could perhaps euphemistically fall under the idea of the disagreeableness of the world to human chauvinism – then Levinas would simply say that this is not to encounter the infinite but the threat of indeterminacy, or of nothing itself. In the final reckoning, the earth may well be strange, but for Levinas it is not irreconcilably strange, not radically other, because we are nevertheless nourished by it until we are not – which is another matter entirely.

The above presents something of a barrier to geologizing human responsibility. Before we attempt to think our way around this it is important to highlight a distinction drawn by Levinas, also in *Totality and Infinity*, between elements and things. Levinas (2007: 139) argues that things can be fixed by the words that communicate them and, as such, remain the same even as they transform. So, for example – and this is Levinas's example – the stone might crumble but we still understand that it is the same stone. More broadly, the world then subsists by being contained in thought, a world where things are given identity by the names that communicate them. Things like stones, then, are not the same as elements like light. There can be a lot of movement here: the forest can become the table and then the table burned becomes smoke; the smoke then leaves the container of thought – it has become elemental. Things are put to work, but the elements are not, because they are indiscernible. But the indiscernible is not without form, and so neither the thing nor the element is in possession of a face, which is formlessness itself.

Whether or not geological entities are things or elements matters, not because it makes a difference to Levinas whether they have a face – neither does – but because the work done by the distinction reveals a further prejudice to Levinas's thought. If Levinas has a concerning attitude towards non-human animals, then it is joined by a suspiciously agricultural account of non-human non-animal existence. According to the distinction, we might say that a rock is a thing, but a lava flow is an element. And from the vantage point of human time this may well be a useful distinction. But in geological time, this is an arbitrary snapshot of a process that stretches backwards and will extend forwards millennia. What will become of the volcanic rock? Many things through human labour, of course, some of which, as we will see shortly, might be beneficial to surviving those other fruits of our labour that have so threatened the environment. The point is that geological entities are always already in process, always already both thing and element, prismatic like that, depending on how we choose to tell the time. Levinas is so focused on human experience, that he is not open to the way that the deep time of geology interrupts and confronts human existence.

We can come at this in a number of ways. Lingis (2019: 22) points to Levinas's first personal approach, arguing that an environment as it appears to me will always then be worked out as an environment that exists for me. He counters this by pointing to the way that the natural world has its own imperative: the routes of rivers that direct me according to their path but also the rocks that obstruct me with their brute massiveness. On this, what of awe, asks Lingis (2019: 24), of the way this magnitude might exceed me and inspire in me a feeling of humility? John Sallis (2010: 91) picks up on Levinas's account of *living from*, by which we assimilate the world through our enjoyment of it, the way that we 'cancel its otherness and affirm its sameness with oneself', but he also raises the possibility that we do not enjoy the world, that its things and its elements alike escape us. Then Boothroyd (2019) wonders if things are really so fixed as this. Nature, he argues, is never a totality, never intact or still; it is stirring, teeming, a 'dynamic interactivity of ... elemental processes' (Boothroyd, 2019: 777). The natural world, Boothroyd (2019: 783) says, 'is the primal scene of totality's breach'. And finally, Cohen (2015: 8) argues that in 'its density, extensiveness, tempo, and force, there is something in rock that is actively unknowable', that the rock does not simply surrender itself to human thought. Levinas's position that the world of things and elements is not radically strange is borne of an artificially still account of the environment, made up of things without time because his time is without things. Thinking of geological time will allow us to accommodate the alterity of rocks set on trajectories of becoming as well as the sublime magnitude of geological breaching, and to recognize a moral universe made up of our temporalities together. That is to say that the task now is to remind ourselves how strange the world is, so that we might then learn to encounter it with the seriousness that strangeness merits.

In making the argument that we should stay on this planet and make good with other entities – non-human and non-animal entities – it has not been the intention to suggest that the surface of the earth is a stable platform for human experience. We should want to reject the inhumanity of Musk or Bezos's designs on space, the dreams of asteroid mines and ex-orbital dwelling, without positing the earth as a stage set for human flourishing. What good that can be done by staying together here on earth is done in full confrontation of what Clark (2005: 179) calls 'the radical contingency of the universe' or what Elizabeth Grosz (2008: 23) identifies as 'cosmological imponderables', those forces that go beyond all human measure. As Clark (2005) argues, there can be resistance to acknowledging this radical contingency, or an aversion to grappling with what is said to be imponderable, because it seems to be at odds with taking responsibility for events – and events that build to and result from climate catastrophe especially. Clark suggests that the singular will always intrude, regardless of human yearning for neat justice; but what we ought to consider, to build on this, is whether the messy or agnostic kind of responsibility we hope to ally to our concern for desertification and extinction and extremity is in fact consummated in this encounter with singularity.

To do so, it is useful to reflect on quite how earth shattering the constitution of the world has always been. Clark highlights the impact of asteroid strikes on evolution, and the way that this reveals the earth to us not as a surface of action but an open system that interacts with the vagaries of the universe. The earth is prone to events that emanate from beyond its atmosphere; this is our 'global ex-orbitance' (Clark, 2005: 166). Human existence is always already interrupted by the encounter with rocks; more than this, human existence is so bound up with such interruptive interaction that it cannot be meaningfully divorced from it.

Back to Levinas (2006b: 74, emphasis in original): 'the Other Person tears me away from my hypostasis, from the *here*, at the heart of being or the centre of the world in which, privileged, and in this sense primordial, I place myself'. We have considered already why Levinas holds this other to be a human other or other person, and so we know why all this talk of privilege and decentring leaves a weak anthropocentrism intact. But this passage also gives an unjustifiably static image of space. We know that time is a movement towards the other, that it has this dynamic moral status for Levinas. I move through time towards the other; I move towards the other through time – but I break with space to do so? I leave it behind? In keeping with Clark's account of the radical contingency of the universe, and with the idea that the geological does not provide a solid ground for human existence, the answer should not only be 'no', it should be instead that it was never mine, that I never did grasp its existence in its entirety, that the 'here' is also other to me. Levinas's approach is a Bergsonian account of time imbued with moral importance, but it repeats the tendency of subordinating space to time that marks a lot of thinking about time-space compression or timeless time or generalized arrival and so on.

By imagining responsibility as a stepping out of the present, where the present is an artificial instant of duration, but also as a stepping out of space, much more broadly conceived, we run the risk, to use the words of Doreen Massey (2005: 7), of 'taming the challenge that the inherent spatiality of the world presents' by imagining it 'as a surface on which we are placed'. Massey gives us an idea of space much more suited to the radical contingency of eruptive and interruptive geological processes, those that emanate from below as well as from the stars above, a space that is a heterogeneous entanglement, rolling and roiling, uneven and ever-changing, a space of overlapping trajectories and multiple durations. Such an imaginary of space is appropriate to our geological understanding; as Clark and Yusoff (2017) argue, the earth is fractured and multiple, a succession of interconnected earths, not a unitary ground but an achievement of many layers.

Massey's (2005: 137) work also reminds us of the way that this teeming earth is on the move at a pace that is its own, of the 'immigrant rocks' that are here now but have been and are nevertheless on their way. We must think here of the continental drift and tectonic activity and the land rising, still, after the weight of the glaciers has been relieved. All this movement, this dynamism, this difference, captured with her allusion to the figure of the immigrant, the stranger, the focus of hospitality and of giving in, say, the work of Derrida (2000b). And this is where the moral importance of space must be given its due. Massey (2005: 140) notes Jean Baudrillard (2010: 3, 5) observing 'the remorseless eternity' of geology in his *America*, where the mountains manifest as 'the immemorial abyss of slowness', but argues that what matters is not, say, the eternity of these hills or this outcrop, or the slowness of that cliff, but the 'throwntogetherness' of space, the challenge of negotiating it, of negotiating encounters with human and non-human and non-human non-animal entities. As Yusoff (2017: 111) points out, geology is both 'extensive and intensive throughout the places of corporeal life'. We do not step out of space when we are being oriented with the other; we are thrown together as we move towards the future. Massey (2005: 140) calls this 'the event of place'. This elusive dynamism, the radical strangeness of the here, evidenced by volcanic cataclysm or the asteroid strike or the unbidden wandering of the stone, reveals the geological as something that is always beyond the human. Levinas would miss this formless exuberance of rocks. The question now is: Can this event also be an encounter with those entities and processes we commonly think of only in terms of their spatiality – the jutting stones and lava flows and the mountains that crumble into rivers towards the seas – that grounds responsibility?

Clark makes a couple of references in his work that seem to hold out hope for this moral encounter being already available. Having established the excessive strangeness of geology, he cites Levinas approvingly for showing how the encounter with the excessive is an opportunity for responsibility that takes us beyond the narrow confines of what we understand to be justice and towards an understanding of a responsibility that is itself excessive (Clark, 2005: 181). Later, with Gormally and Tuffen, he draws our attention to Maurice Blanchot's description of our exposure to the face not only as excessive, but also as coming face to face with 'the magma of the other' (in Clark, Gormally and Tuffen, 2018: 290). But the magma of the other is not automatically reversible; that is, it is not straightforwardly the case that the magmatic is an other to whom I respond magnanimously through giving. If magma here figuratively picks out the excessiveness of the other then it remains to be seen if there is an otherness to literal magma or other geological entities. We have seen already, through examinations of Levinas's humanism and of his exclusion of animals, that an excess is not enough to have a face; that the other must be something that can be touched but not grasped; and that the relationship to the other is speech. If we are to say that we encounter geological entities as an event of responsibility then we need to establish that such encounters are a kind of contact with the singular – haptic, communicative, yes, but moral above all.

To complicate things further, Levinas himself has some choice things to say about rocks and things in general, many of which metaphorical but that, in their use, reveal a certain disposition towards the lithic that is, at the very least, ungenerous. In 'Is Ontology Fundamental?' Levinas (1996: 10) asks: 'Can things take on a face?' This comes at the end of an argument that the only relation that cannot be reduced to the same through comprehension is the relation to the other. He concludes, on whether things face us, that his 'analysis thus far does not suffice for an answer' (Levinas, 1996: 10). This is a very good answer, and it is not obvious that Levinas's attempts to go farther were an improvement on this kind of *agnosticism of every other thing*. But he does go on, with literal and metaphorical reference to stone, and it provides an opportunity to think, with and against Levinas, the encounter with the geological. He says, in 'Language and Proximity', that the tenderness of the human touch and the touching human is in stark contrast with the 'cold' and 'mineral' contact that is 'congealed into pure information' (Levinas, 2006a: 119). We see here then that allusions to stone stand in for the kind of encounter we have in relations that can be reduced to the comprehensible – and we can note further that this is not out of kilter with the operating logic of geological science that would know the world in possessive and extractive fashion. That is, Levinas is right, we do claim to coldly reduce the geological to information, but this should not fix what geological entities can be or how we ought to approach them.

In places it is as if Levinas wants to resist the imperialism of metaphysics apart from where it is left very much in place to motivate the distinction between the otherness of the other and the sameness of non-humans. This construct is at work in 'Ethics and Spirit' when he considers the constellation of violence and speech. Levinas (1997: 6) writes: 'Violence is to be found in any action in which one acts as if we are alone to act: as if the rest of the universe were there only to *receive* the action; violence is consequently also any action which we endure without at every point collaborating in it.' In which case, almost every action is violent. But then only language as saying – the 'banal fact of conversation' (Levinas, 1997: 7) as greeting the other – is said to be non-violence. Surely, if almost every action is violence – because it is said to be undertaken as if the universe were there to receive my actions – then there is more at stake than the human other? Potentially we get more from the statement above, about a responsibility to the universe that holds even to omission, a responsibility fit, it would seem, for an Anthropocene, but it is taken away if we cannot greet the stone or converse the rock. That said, we know from our account of saying animals that there is more to saying than sounds and so there is the possibility that a stony silence may also be a conversation. Levinas (2007: 91) writes that 'silence is not a simple absence of speech; speech lies in the depths of silence like a laughter perfidiously held back'. So: we need to ask what the stone holds back; we need to think about whether the stone touched is revealed or resists; and we need first to ensure an otherness to the geological that does justice to its strange excess.

Geolterity

Edward Casey (2003: 201–3) suggests that there is a possibility that the environment itself presents to us a face, that we might catch a glimpse of this face when we experience the wellness or illness of the environment. He writes:

> The environment turns a face to us from within its many surfaces: not the infinite and transcendent enigmatic Other's face of such high priority for Levinas but an immanent, intense faciality of its own, one in which we can discern stress without having to make it analogous to human suffering. (Casey, 2003: 204)

In response to Casey it should be said that there really should not be an idea of 'the face for Levinas', not least because he claimed not to know whether certain entities had a face, or because, as Derrida (2008: 109) suggested, Levinas did not know what the face was at all, but also, more positively, because it should be an open question what can approach me with a face. This is in line with the agnosticism that Calarco has impressed upon this present work. Can things or elements have an enigmatic transcendence? In the case of geological entities, we might say that they present their extensive and intensive magnitude as events of tranascendence *and* transdescendence: the interruptive excess of the volcanic or the seismic *and* the grounding excess of the geological deep time that binds us with processes beyond human time and immediate experience; the height from which these events escape me *and* the vulnerability of the geological system that demands from me the gift of care. We might also say, in response to Casey, that the idea of an environment having a face across multiple surfaces is much less appealing, in light of Massey's direction, than positing instead infinite faces that pick out the contingency of an environment made up by singular entities, each of which are more than that environment they co-author. As Llewellyn (1991: 266–7) points out, it is to a singularity and not a general concept that I am responsible, and this has to be the case if we are to work from an account of responsibility that fashions it as a break from totality.

Levinas would say that the human is non-interchangeable, such that when I substitute myself for the others by assuming my responsibility without concern for theirs, the otherness of the other remains intact. Animals, as we know, are for Levinas the kinds of entities that are interchangeable; when I encounter a chicken, it makes little difference whether it is this chicken or that. Of course, it does, if my responsibility is directed towards the vulnerability of a given animal, since suffering, as an attack on individual existence, is never shared, even when it is synchronous; and it does if it is my murderousness that the face resists with its saying no. When we talk about environmental catastrophe then this question of interchangeability takes on a new urgency. When species become extinct then it will be too late to reflect on how blasé a stance it is to say that this animal is like that one. This extinction is not the disappearance of a mass, but the attrition of singular entities taken from the world.

We are familiar with worries about the non-renewable, about the removal of carbon from the ground and its release into the atmosphere, although too often this reflects our clinging on to fossil fuels, a fear of running out rather than of CO_2 running over and strangling the world. And we worry too of the ice caps melting, knowing of course that we cannot put them back – although beneath this those still clinging might find fleetingly the fossil fuels they have been after all along. What about rocks? Is not this rock much like the other? When we touch the rock and when we communicate with the rock, we might find that this is not the case. But even before that we can say that our relationship to the deep time of geology means that we have responsibilities to the specific rock. The slow carbonation process of weathering, by which CO_2 is removed from the atmosphere and then buried as stones break down, ties the individual rock we navigate in the encounter to the vitality of the world. The extension of this one rock, the way it takes up space and then, by weathering, takes up space differently, ties it into the intensity of a world not given to me but irreplaceable in its being. This irreplaceability means one thing above all others: that the wellness of the outside is the wellness of the interior; the sickness of the world collides with a sickness in me. In a finite world, the death of the animal or the melting of the ice or the disregard for the geologic is the death of humanity in some linear sense, yes, but really, the encounter with environmental catastrophe is simply a catching up with the death of the human held in abeyance. We can hold ourselves accountable for the very worst, the destruction of this geological alterity, this *geolterity*, or cheat ourselves and die in vain.

But do rocks suffer? Casey is right that we should not look to analogy with the human here; it would undermine singular suffering in all directions to compare the hardship of the stone to that of the human – but more than this, such things are incommensurable in any case. We cannot measure vulnerability and calculate our response. There is no computational responsibility. A rock is not like a human. But the whole point with Levinas is that this human is not like this other human. This other human is not like me. Responsibility does not seek its own reflection. And if things cannot be more other than other (recall the discussion of Derrida and his claims to this effect for animals) then for all it matters the igneous is to me as the strange fellow. Geolterity is ultimately an alterity like any other, which is to say, unlike any other but given its specificity, a uniqueness worth naming since it is too readily denied to it. Llewelyn (1991: 263) reinforces this point when he reminds us that responsibility is not a matter of degree; it is a confrontation with something so fundamentally aloof from me that it humbles me – and ought to enthuse me and pull me towards it.

But Llewelyn only takes us so far. His arguments about giving in the context of geology are poignant and vital. Llewelyn (1991: 269) argues that things are not simply what are given to us. Nor are things simply what are to be given to others. Things must be given respect. They must be afforded the gift of being let be. Using the example of a rock, Llewelyn (1991: 270) says that letting it be would mean that we should not grind it into dust. Or rather, he ultimately says that what matters with regards to what we do with things is that we do them with care, such that pulverizing the rock as pure vandalism would be careless but that the rock can still be put to use. The problem here is that it is not on the face of it obvious that grinding a rock down dramatically changes its way of being, and there is a faint suggestion here that a prohibition against the needless grinding of rocks leans too heavily both on an idea of utility and on a human sense of integrity. The argument to come will be that if we embrace non-integral, non-human ways of being then we can make better arguments against wanton vandalism of rocks (or plants) that still allow for their cultivation and utilization, but this is best served if we first continue on our way to the matter of touching rocks.

When we touch the rock, although we might grasp it in our hands, we are unable fully to assimilate it to our needs. Klaver (2003: 161), in making an argument about the geological basis of human culture, writes: 'Stone endures, bears weight, withstands the elements.' It does, of course, but in ways that bear more seriously, or primarily, on the moral status of rocks and not the geological constitution of culture. The rock takes up space and when I hold it, it does so much more than withhold its internal space from the occupation of my touch. Lingis (2019: 23) argues that non-human non-animal entities have needs. The rock needs the space it occupies just as the river needs the banks that delimit its course. In touching the rock my hands become a shoreline. My extent is limited by the presence of the stone encountered by my skin. We can say this of any object, yes, but that is a different business and would require some account of its singular strangeness just as we have, already, an understanding of the rock's geolterity. The weight of the stone, its gravity, its moral pull on me, is not the weight of my geologic culture; it is not derived from the simple fact of its endurance through time; and it does not rely on its withstanding of the elements. The weight of the rock is found in its transcendental ascendence and descendance, the magnitude of its own time, beyond human measurement, its duration, and the way that it is here, but not in my site, not forming my ground but shifting and migrating, its co-constitution of a heterogeneous environment that is not so much a surface as up in the air, that rises and weathers and erupts. It is the human that the rock withstands.

To emphasize the primacy of geology's moral gravity above its cultural interpolation is not to say that the weight of human history does not bear down on it. In fact, it does so in ways that ought to reinforce our responsibility to the rock. In her account of geology and colonialism, Yusoff (2018a) argues that the science of geology – what we might differentiate from geological entities and processes as *human ways of seeing the geological* – is, as an extractive and classificatory system, a technology of empire that exhausts places and prioritizes and reproduces whiteness. Levinas cannot oppose totality or resist the imperialism of the same by traducing the rock (or the animal or the elements) by the logic of a project of anti-blackness on the grounds that it is, at the very least, inconsistent with openness to the other (even if geologic entities are not considered to possess otherness). That is, any totality allowed to stand *a priori* rules out in advance an encounter with otherness that might come to be revealed. We can only claim to know the rock, to measure it and so possess it first by cognition and then by violence, if we ignore all evidence of its resistance. The rock when touched is not congealed into information; we merely act as if it is: the coldness belongs to our way of touching and not to the stone itself. In the course of human time, it might appear that the rock can be mastered; beyond this, the claim is absurd – and reveals that it is absurd no matter what snapshot of duration is taken. We can touch the stone or we can grasp it; to do the latter justified by the argumentation of Levinas would be to accept the rules of the game and cheat anyway.

The rock communicates its otherness by touch but the very possibility of this kind of encounter necessitates that the rock is always already in conversation with me. Life is a constant negotiation with the geological world. In the rocky environ, negotiating often connotes mastery, as when a difficult pass is negotiated in mountaineering. This idea of conquering the natural world lends itself to an account of responsibility that sees the human step outside the environment when it overcomes nature and the struggle for its own existence to give to the other. Levinas (2008b: 8) argues in *Otherwise than Being* that when we go beyond essence we break with the question of the where, that responsibility is enacted in a 'null site' or 'non-lieu'. Here Levinas is not speaking of the same spatiality as Marc Augé (2008); for Augé non-places are stripped of anthropological meaning whereas for Levinas the non-lieu would be the height of humanity as responsibility, or rather, responsibility as a response to the height of the other. The kinds of sites Augé is concerned with are constituted not by their withdrawal from the human but by the overwhelming sameness of their voice (see Hill and Martin, 2017). These are environments without hidden depth. They are spaces that act as mirrors, reflecting back human desire. These non-places do not speak to me because they do not need to. Alterity demands negotiation; the sameness of the non-place need only be silent. Artifice brings us to this muted state, but in the geological world there is much to say. An understanding of space as a teeming heterogeneity requires constant attention. This world withdraws from me with every step I take towards it. I am constantly playing catch up, never mastering, always moving towards and never fully in its site. If the Augéan non-place resides in the said, then the natural environment is encountered in saying. We could never step outside it to a Levinasian non-lieu because this would refuse its alterity and because we were never really in it to begin with. We are, more precisely, *with* the geological, *towards* the world.

To be with the world means to be in conversation with it, to listen and respond, to be drawn out from ourselves and towards an environment that does not centre on me, that does not envelop me, but that moves me in its direction. Conversation so understood is not to broadcast to the other, to fill the world up with me, but to step back from myself and towards the other in a stance of attentive listening (see Hill, 2020a). It means to be open to the other whatever the other may say or how this saying is undertaken. That demand to pay attention to the other, to patiently allow for the other to say to me what they will, unhindered by my own totalizing talk, is so fundamentally part of my encounter with otherness that the responsibility to listen holds even when confronted with the stoniest of silences.

Llewelyn (2010: 107) argues that not having a voice means that those who can speak must speak up, for the voiceless, such that any ecological ethics would demand that responsibility is directed towards non-human non-animal entities that suffer anthropogenic climate change silently. But this talk of speaking up sits uncomfortably within the confines of Levinasian response. When I speak for the other I speak over the other, I construct the other in my language and fill them up with myself. To emphasize listening is to instead recognize that non-human non-animal entities have their own needs; I might not always hear them, but I must listen out; I might not always meet those needs when I think I respond responsibly but I must try to act with fidelity to what is communicated. As Cohen (2015: 249) writes: 'Stones are rich in worlds not ours, while we are poor in their duration. We therefore have a terrible problem communicating with each other.' And yet still we do, still we communicate, we make the attempt, out of love, says Cohen, out of what he calls *geophilia*, but really, we should say, out of responsibility. The problem with the way that Levinas conceives of the environment is not that the human does not speak for the non-human but that the human is excused from hearing the non-human. We should rectify this not by amplifying the human voice but by acknowledging the language of stone, the saying of the geologic experienced in our negotiation of their spatiality.

Geological giving

If we want to defend a kind of 'geologic communization' (Yusoff, 2016: 8) – that is, to open up a radical space in which we are with geological entities and processes – then it must be founded on communication: giving a voice to the stone, lending an ear, paying attention. Moral gravity so understood, as being here with the geologic and the animal and the human and so on, is not just a pulling but also a giving, a gift to the other. Only when we hear the rock are we in a position to encounter it. Only when we give to the rock without expectation of what use it has to me can we be in a relationship with the world. This kind of encounter is characterized by Manuel Tironi (2019: 287) as 'geo-affective'. We might say that in this relationship I am first moved by the rock and then move towards it, orient myself to its being, step out of myself and in its direction through the gesture of giving as an event of responsibility.

Are we moved by rocks? Do we find in this encounter a welcome? Do we give such a welcome? Tironi (2019: 294) argues that the inhospitality of the rocky environment seems to intensify our enjoyment with it, as we persevere to stay alongside the radical otherness of an environment that cannot simply be assimilated to my needs, that I am in proximity with not based on connection but on the abutment of our radically divergent existences. Tironi makes this case through a reading of Levinas and, while we need to be careful of how far we go from enjoyment to responsibility, particularly whether this enjoyment picks out being with or merely being alongside, to the extent that it would be useful not to build from the enjoyment of the mountain or the challenge of the terrain as something to be thrilled to, Tironi gives us a vital conception of the relationship to geology as a 'partial companionship' (Tironi, 2019: 297). Geological entities resist and withdraw; when I am with the geologic it is relentless in its indifference to me no matter how I try to interact with it. A partial companionship, then, doomed always to be incomplete, a perpetual movement of me to this geolterity, never arriving, always listening but never really understanding. The geologic is not grasped by me; it evades me utterly, transcends me from above and from below, compels me, pacifically, to give over to it.

Of course, we do not always give geological entities their own space. We blow them up when they are in our way, sculpt them in our own image and, as Levinas says, grind them to dust. But what if our ability to stay together, here, all of us – the human and the animal and the plant and the elemental and the geologic – meant that we had to transform the spatial dimensions of the rock with some moral urgency? Would that be violence? Is it permissible to sacrifice the stone to the others? Holly Buck (2019: 141–52), while cautioning against altering the reflectivity of the earth – bouncing sunlight into space to stymy warming – examines more positively the potential for accelerated weathering. This would entail grinding stones and spreading them on fields, accelerating the process by which rocks are weathered and thereby burying CO_2 much sooner than if uninterrupted. Our licence to embark on such activity, if such an activity is warranted, is not that it is for the good of abstract entities called humans or animals or plants to reduce the singular rock to smithereens, since the logic here is barbarous if, as we have been arguing, responsibility is due without prejudice or predetermination, but rather that the rock does not suffer the process because rock has the kind of existence that bears its weathering. This is an argument made clearer with reference to plant being.

Levinas has said that the human is not in vegetable communication with the elements, is not, by the dwelling, rooted into the ground, and he has other choice words to valorize the human and denigrate plant life too. In 'Ethics and Spirit' he writes: 'Consciousness is the impossibility of invading reality like a wild vegetation that absorbs or breaks or pushes back everything around it' (Levinas, 1997: 9). Levinas is here suggesting that only the human can resist the violence of acting as if the universe was there to receive them. While it seems odd to suggest that humans are unique among entities in their ability to step back from colonizing the world, it makes sense according to the logic of his work, even if it is ultimately found to be wrong. That is to say, if morality is human, and if morality means a break from nature, then it makes sense to say that the human might resist the desire to invade reality while wild vegetation undertakes it as a matter of course. But, of course, we should reject this attempt to delimit what morality is, or who it might encompass, not least because it allows us to avoid the following: Levinas (1997: 9) says that morality 'is the fact of not existing violently or naturally', so equating violence to nature, while also holding that violence is the human taking possession of the world. We should want to resist the position that violence is something humans undertake when they are acting unlike humans, which is to say without responsibility, not least of all because it is counterintuitive and profligate as far as explanations go. We should want to retain the option of saying that human violence is a distinctly human mode of existing towards the world so that we can then take this stance morally seriously when the harm caused, and suffering endured, belongs to the world.

To do this, we would also need to show that being wild vegetation is simply a different, or, rather, a radically other, and not a lesser way of being. Levinas (1997: 100) would close off this option when, in 'Place and Utopia', he traduces vegetal life with his remarks on 'being a man–plant': 'What is an individual, a solitary individual, if not a tree that grows without regard for everything it supresses and breaks, grabbing all the nourishment, air and sun, a being that is fully justified in its nature and its being?'

The argument made by Levinas is that responsibility snaps us out of a plant-like existence, moves us on in time and out of the ground, away from ourselves and towards the other. It rests on an idea that the human is morally capable of attention to others where other entities invade and hog and crowd out. The human steps out of place whereas the tree takes up space. This distinction rests on an understanding that the human has a dwelling as an opening to the world, from where ventures out and welcomes in are organized, whereas the non-human is grounded in the elements. To prize this open it will not do to claim that the tree has its dwelling, since we cannot know the tree. But if we lean into this agnosticism and see that we cannot know if the plant has a face, that it is discovered in the encounter, then we can say that the tree should be allowed its space, just as we should want to say that the rock might have its space. Calarco (2015: 42) is clear that the ethics of difference that subtends his reading of Levinas would have to extend to plants for just this reason; you cannot foreclose in advance which encounters are encounters with responsibility. And if the rock should be given its space because its deep time and uncanny migration is encountered as a *geolterity* then we will see now that the tree has its *vegetalterity* as a result of its own being in time, and that this should instruct us as to the moral status of the integrity of the rock.

To make this case it is worth taking a sustained look at Michael Marder's work on plant being. In his rich account of vegetal life Marder (2013: 4) observes that the 'sheer strangeness' of plants means we see nothing of our humanity in them, but that, when we cultivate and instrumentalize plants – a field of cereal, say – we do not encounter the strangeness of the plant and therefore do not encounter the plant itself. The human relationship to plants is then arranged so that the strangeness of their individual being is rendered invisible by the totalizing force of human activity. But this invisibility is not without its gesture; speech, as we know, cuts across vision, resists, from a position of weakness, my totalizing tendencies – even in silence. What does the plant say? Marder (2013: 74) argues that the plant is speechless, that it cannot address us, that the silence of the plant does not conceal or hold anything back because it cannot be otherwise than silent. Instead, the plant gestures spatially; it moves, it orients itself, it reveals its need in this orientation. In which case, *pace* Marder, we should say that the plant says, that it is not at all silent, that the real silence resides in the said, in the broadcast of speech, whereas this gesture, this saying, that demands attention to divine this need and orient ourselves to its pacific demand, brings us into conversation with plant life and confrontation with plant being. For Marder (2013: 186), the plant's speechlessness makes it subaltern, and then we might be tempted to say that here is its vulnerability that I tend to, that I meet with my responsibility, but then lots of things are quiet: what matters is whether or not they have something to say. Instead we should hold that the plant's need to take up space and orient itself, in the sun's direction and, since it needs my help, in my direction, is the source of its vulnerability, that it is my hearing this or not that makes it subaltern, since either way it needs me to hear, and that my responsibility is then to listen to the plant and respond to the call of its being. With these adjustments in mind, a turn to Marder will show us the way to geological giving.

Marder (2013: 187) argues that when it comes to consideration of whether something has the status of a moral entity, what matters is that it has finitude and not that it has sentience. That something will come to an end, and that its existence is given shape by this, is for Marder more salient than its knowing this to be the case. This is not to say that the end of the plant is analogous to the death of the human. Marder (2013: 72) approaches this difference when he asks whether plants are part of the elemental environment or whether they have their own temporality that cannot be reduced to a simple spatial dimension. And he has a good answer: 'The hetero-temporality of vegetal existence is the most telling instantiation of the ethical injunction for openness to the other. The plant's future is entirely contingent on alterity when it comes to the process of ripening, the possibilities of flourishing and withering away, and so forth' (Marder, 2013: 107).

That being the case, however, means that what matters is not so much the plant's finitude but, in Levinasian terms, its 'fecundity': where an openness to alterity gives birth to the future (see Levinas, 2007: 268). Marder says that the plant in its contingency exists in a stance of exposure more passive than all passivity. But in its reliance on me and on others the question of the plant's existence is posed most pressingly not by its finitude but by this very recourse, by its vulnerability, by its suffering and its openness to the actions of its exterior. Perhaps we might say that the plant is altogether too passive to its lot in life to warrant moral attention. Here Marder (2013: 69) cautions that such would be a human projection, that the plant is neither passive nor active, that it goes beyond this binary container, possessing a radical or moral passivity that escapes definition. To be so open to the elements, to be so given over to the other, opposes human ideas of what it is to exist so totally that it resists the totalizing project of the human, leaving the plant beyond, outside, above human existence. And with such an entity it is only possible to have an infinite relation, which is to say, a moral relation, an encounter predicated on responsive and sensitive giving.

Marder (2013: 132) argues that we demean this passivity, this 'vegetal indifference', because it is incompatible with the human notion of existing towards death as an existence organized as projects or as authorship. We know, however, that Levinas does not, that passivity is at the heart of his humanism of the other, the way that the human is interrupted by the other and then disregards their own needs so completely in their going over to the other. We then only need to ensure that we do not demean this plant passivity when a radicalization of responsibility would venerate human passivity.

How can a plant that will simply blow in the wind make its mark on the world? The plant drops its leaves, is eaten by animals and trampled by humans. What manner of life is this, that so completely jolts the fullness of being, the integrity of existence? What if, asks Marder (2013: 135), the plant falling apart – not remaining intact, spreading its seeds far – is simply a different kind of engagement in the world, one marked by an 'ontological indifference to being' itself? Then we would need to extend responsibility to plants without tying it to empathy or reducing it to sympathy. We would need to act with responsibility to the temporality of plants, which would mean to not impose human ideas of integrity and activity to them. And then we could blow the dandelions and eat the spinach leaves and powder the turmeric roots and still let these things be, since their existence is the kind of thing that embraces these relationships with others. The plant propagates its being, reproduces itself in the world, in ways that are not analogous to the human or the animal. The trick is to let them be, to reject totally the human vandalism of their environment, or the toxicity of our instrumentality with regards to plants, without, by pegging it to human existentiality, losing sight of – or really, without falling deaf to – how they need to be in the world.

Finally, then, we can make, by extension of Marder, our fullest case for the strange moral gravity of geological entities and processes. The rock is not speechless. It communicates with me by its own spatial presence, and I ought to respond with fidelity to that being in the world by moving in its direction and by letting it be. Yes, the rock suffers. It suffers and it suffers me. It suffers and its suffering will reach into the future. Human activity guarantees it. Human activity worsens it. But that suffering is not analogous to human suffering. We can make no sense of it by recourse to human ideas of psychological integrity or bodily autonomy, nor by psychological autonomy or bodily integrity. As Cohen (2015: 256) points out, we only think that the stone persists in one state because in this state it outlasts us. The rock is open to the elements, more passive than passivity itself in its being given over to its weathering. And yet it is also, in this regard, prone to me, and to my regard, but outside me and my totalizing intentions, and therefore transcendent and morally serious. We have today forced the geological to reside in human time. As Yusoff (2016: 11–12) observes, the Anthropocene threatens human existence because it is such a disastrous intervention into the constitution of the human by geological deep time. Whereas before the Anthropocene geological temporality exceeded the human, now human activity changes the geological record. But this is not, as Yusoff suggests, a collapse of the division between geologic time and human temporality; it is a failed imperialism, a colonization of what is proper to the geological that highlights only further the urgency of the opposition of the geologic to the human, a pacific opposition that demands we act responsibly towards it. It is failed because it destroys us all.

Can we grind up the rocks to geoengineer a more habitable planet for humans and rocks and plants and animals and everything that is bound to this earth? Without certainty, yes. The rock is the kind of thing that exists with its weathering, not towards a death, not as finitude, but as an entity indifferent to its own integrity. This accelerated weathering would allow the rock to be as it is in the world, open, indifferently, to the elements and to others. It wants to be indifferently to the others and cannot so be without the others. Preserving life on this planet in such a way preserves the existence of the rock. Because ultimately the rock cannot reside indifferently towards the others without those others. Its indifference is predicated on a non-indifference to the existence of the others to whom it is indifferent. It is not radically passive without all of us here, together; otherwise, the rock would be simply alone – and then it loses its fecundity. As such, we should not vandalize the rock, not because it has a higher purpose or a project of its own, but because we are responsible with it to give birth to a future habitable to all.

The important thing is not so much about whether this or that is prohibited – we find responsibility together in the encounter – but that we encounter the geological without ignoring its otherness and without anthropomorphizing its existence. As Yusoff (2015: 388) argues, we have to avoid the idea that encounters with geologic entities add to the human. Our relationship with the geological has to be something between us and not a renewal of human ascendancy. Yusoff advises that we do not need to settle what this is between us, but instead to learn to inhabit it and to dismantle the boundary between the geologic and the biologic. But if there is not a boundary then there is still a chasm, an abyss of otherness that cannot be jumped across. We take a step in its direction, nonetheless. We step towards the abyss without self-concern – without self-preservation. The best chance we have of preserving life on earth is to abandon the idea of moral gravity as a human preserve and risk ourselves for the others, the other ones and the other things. Peter Singer (2012) observes that for Levinas, animals and plants and rocks are all to be encountered phenomenologically as things but that the implications of his work can suggest a more generous kind of encounter. This generosity should mean giving the non-human non-animal other its space, giving it our attention that we might hear its silent speech, and then giving everything we have to ensure that its strangely indifferent and radically passive existence in the world is secured.

Lithic gravity

Are we then supposed to turn into rocks? Singer (2012) reminds us of Heidegger's similar rejoinder to Nietzsche and his attempts to valorize the animal. Of course, one day, we may find ourselves as fossils. Or others will find us that way as we exist beyond passivity, otherwise than human, no longer finding but still being or being still, still in need or prone to the vagaries of a world we suffer. As Vannini and Vannini (2020) argue, the fossil evokes the presence of life but also its absence in the present; it is restless in its resistance to obliteration, active in its leaving of a trace, dynamic in its transformation into something other than its previous state. Human fossils would still be sociable entities. Until then, it has been our purpose to recognize the rock as rock, as strange and transcendent, rather than to assimilate it to me or to cavort in its image.

Human existence is bound up with but exceeded by the geologic; human temporality and the deep time of geology are partners in a dance that moves towards the future, touching but separate, and moving only where there is care and attention and responsibility. We are not at home in the world and we do not step outside the natural environment when we encounter the other; the geologic creates an unstable, moving, open world, and we must move carefully towards this *here* that is radically strange and that always steps away. This carefulness is a kind of communication with geolterity, an attentiveness to the presentation of the face that communicates its strangeness to me and therefore its vulnerability to me. What the rock says must be responded to by giving it my attention but also its space and its future. This is our being with geology, which is to say, the fecundity of a relationship with geological entities and processes that might give us a future we can all live with. Taken together, we have an account that gives a face to geology, that recognizes that the geological suffers, that it has what Cohen (2015: 133) calls its 'lithic gravity', the way it draws us to it, which is really a moral gravity consummated in responsibility before it is bound in love. As Llewelyn (1991: 269) concludes, if in human ethics the face of the other is human, then in ecological ethics it can be, without contradiction, non-human. We do not turn into rocks; we turn, are turned towards the face of the rock and then refuse to turn a deaf ear to its suffering.

If this sounds altogether absurd, then some solace can be found in Calarco's observation that the whole point of thinking with Levinas is to go beyond reason and what is reasonable. He writes that 'any thought worthy of the name, especially any thought of *ethics*, takes its point of departure in setting up a critical relation to common sense and the established *doxa*' (Calarco, 2008: 72, emphasis in original). Then we have an idea of responsibility to others in line with Judith Butler's concern for the precarity of all existence. 'Ethics', Butler (2016: 181) writes, 'is less a calculation than something that follows from being addressed and addressable in sustainable ways'. When we unreasonably grant to the rock the status of an entity that suffers, or rather, when we concede beyond reason that when we encounter the rock it communicates to us its suffering, we face the rock with humility. When we turn enthusiastically in the rock's direction, we face a future together that is more sustainable. We can only do this by doing away with calculation, by recognizing that geological entities and processes exceed the human, that they are incomparably other to me. Our humanism of the other reaches out to the non-human animal and the non-human non-animal being.

My responsibility to others is a human responsibility but I do not limit it to humans nor decide whether or not non-human others might extend it to me. This marks the accession of the non-human to our moral universe, and we accede to the needs of everyone and everything if we are to have a world worth staying for and worth living with.

End

There is no satisfying end to a book that calls for a revolution in morality. Its conceptual activism simply opens on to the practical work of finding a way to live together well into the future. This environmentalism of precarious lives can find its expression only in encounter and community; it is not to be found here, somehow, at the end, but in the future we build by taking seriously all others and orienting ourselves to them, by listening and then acting together in radical renunciation of the present. The response to environmental catastrophe, which we know is here but also still to come, has not been said – it is found in saying.

It has been the position of this book that we find little hope of the right response if we refuse to find others and if we refuse to find a moral seriousness at large in the world. Beginning with hopelessness we see that the only way forward is to move out towards the most vulnerable, to see death as collective in such a way that every individual loss is an inexcusable tragedy that demands a responsibility that extends across distance and difference and that embraces the other. In such an embrace we find cause to resist the schemes of those personifications of capital that would shoot us to the moon or to Mars, wrenching human experience from the world that nourishes it and from the non-human existences that enrich it, and reducing what the human can mean to a portable freight unanchored from its most vital meaning making. Staying together here is only then sustainable if those others we are bound up with are non-human others also. It would mean finding moral seriousness where it presents itself, in the face of the animal or the geolterity of the stone – or the vegetalterity of the plant or the excession of the elemental. When we are attentive to all others, when we take seriously the moral claims they make of us without prejudice or predetermination, and when we are moved by their vulnerability and so move in their direction in a gesture of giving, our revolution in morality is underway. After that, an environmentalism of precarious lives is something that is to be found out there and in those encounters.

We arrived at this possibility by embarking on a sociology of the very worst, not as a programme, not as a disciplinarity turned towards disaster, but as a mood – of thought, of being – that looks for the duplex undoing of the human, the catastrophe that attends the organization of our atomized societies and the small good of the intersubjective that shatters our solitary existence and takes us out towards the other. To be a social being is a disaster; or at least, we have to hope so. We have to be undone to find the future.

A final question: Why Levinas if it has taken us to such lengths to imagine his thought fit for animals and plants and rocks and so on? Why with and against Levinas when we could drink from less polluted streams? We have seen that Levinas gives us an idea of responsibility that is for the vulnerable and the precarious; that is beyond reason and calculation; that is grounded in the world of encounters; and that must be agnostic about what it encounters. This gives us an idea of moral gravity that cannot be denied to the other person or to the other animal; an understanding of responsibility that must now extend to geological entities and processes; that could even now be shown to reach out to the light and the tides and soils. Levinas gives us call to stay together here on earth with an account of responsibility that would make that life here rich in experience and full in relation. Our existence would then be truly life-sized.

To live otherwise than being, an existence that takes seriously that of all others and reaches out to them with a careful touch and an open ear, is urgent when we survey our environmental catastrophe. At the same time, we must be patient. The road forward together demands attention to local experience, to multiple voices, to muted suffering. Fucking off to Mars is an unnecessary haste to the extent that it defaults to the path already taken, trodden into the world by the dominance of society's speed-mongers. We reject this rush not by reluctance to act but by enthusiasm for the other. The patience we require is not a slowness or delay but a refusal to act without confronting the seriousness of the other. Without it we might take a giant leap away from our planet and not a single step into the future. And then we are left again masquerading in the present, however quickly we shoot up past the earth's pull. What we need, and what we find for the final time now in Levinas, is a kind of *urgent patience.*

We have seen that Levinas presents responsibility as a kind of passivity, or an exposure, to be open to the other, exposed to their saying, open to the outrage of their suffering and myself open to a world that will commit outrages against me, and nevertheless to put the other before my freedom, 'a passivity more passive than all passivity' (2008b: 15), a passivity that does not hold back despite what will come. This passivity is to substitute myself for the others, to be otherwise than being. Why me? 'To be reduced to having recourse to me', writes Levinas (2008b: 91), 'is the homelessness or strangeness of the neighbour. It is incumbent on me.' This is all the more urgent if we are to make short our Anthropocene, when human temporality opposes the deep time of geology, if only in the moment, if only ever in futility, a forlorn opposition that is shown in all its hubris when set against its engulfment by the catastrophe set in train. This outrage demands urgency, but not without patience. Patience, as Levinas (2008d: 134–5) explains in his essay 'The Old and the New', is part of responsibility. Grasping at things is impatience; deferring to the other – and not taking hold of their otherness and encompassing it – can only be patient. Being with means listening attentively, allowing the other to say and to show and to reveal what it can. Responsibility is all the more urgent because it demands patience. Anything else would overwhelm the needs of the other. We must be more passive, substitute ourselves for the planet that is harmed, listen patiently to the world so we know how to respond, and tend to those in need, however they present their face to us, as a matter of existential exigency.

In staying together at the end of the world we stay together not in contemplation of the end of the world but to bring the world to an end. Kathryn Yusoff (2018a: 104) rejects the very possibility of a moral thought that would make the world better and calls instead for moral thought suitable to begin a new world. In Levinasian terms, our revolution in morality would be a tearing from, to tear the human from this world, a world of possession, and our possession of a world of things, and to instead throw us into a new world where we are with non-human animals and non-animal entities, to be now with a world that is totally strange, but because of this strangeness, because of this world's retreat from me, a world that I can move towards, and move forwards with into a future that is hospitable to all. The new world we need is not to be found beyond the earth's orbit or the sun's light. It is a new world insofar as we experience it subject to a new moral gravity, which was always already there, such that the human 'answers for that which his intentions have encompassed' (Levinas, 1997: 295), and does so with an urgent patience, instead of responding with unhearing power to the suffering of everyone and everything.

In the end, there, perhaps, is the sustainability of our future together.

References

Angus, I. (2016) *Facing the Anthropocene: Fossil Capitalism and the Crisis of the Earth System*, New York: Monthly Review Press.

Atterton, P. (2012) 'Ethical cynicism', in P. Atterton and M. Calarco (eds) *Animal Philosophy: Ethics and Identity*, London: Continuum, pp 51–61.

Atterton, P. (2019) 'Dog philosophy: does Bobby have what it takes to be moral?', in P. Atterton and T. Wright (eds) *Face to Face with Animals: Levinas and the Animal Question*, New York: SUNY Press, pp 63–89.

Augé, M. (2008) *Non-Places: An Introduction to Supermodernity*, London: Verso.

Bataille, G. (1985) *Visions of Excess: Selected Writings, 1927–1939*, trans. A. Stoekl, Minneapolis: University of Minnesota Press.

Baudrillard, J. (2010) *America*, trans. C. Turner, London: Verso.

Bignall, S. and Braidotti, R. (2019) 'Posthuman systems', in R. Braidotti and S. Bignall (eds) *Posthuman Ecologies: Complexity and Process after Deleuze*, London: Rowman & Littlefield, pp 1–16.

Blanchot, M. (1989) *The Space of Literature*, trans. A. Smock, London: University of Nebraska Press.

Blanchot, M. (1995) *The Writing of the Disaster*, trans. A. Smock, London: University of Nebraska Press.

Blanchot, M. (2000) *The Instant of my Death*, trans. E. Rottenberg, Stanford: Stanford University Press.

Bonneuil, C. and Fressoz, J-B. (2017) *The Shock of the Anthropocene: The Earth, History and Us*, trans. D. Fernbach, London: Verso.

Boothroyd, D. (2019) 'Levinas on ecology and nature', in M.L. Morgan (ed) *The Oxford Handbook of Levinas*, Oxford: Oxford University Press, pp 769–88.

Buck, H.J. (2019) *After Geoengineering: Climate Tragedy, Repair, and Restoration*, London: Verso.

Butler, J. (2006) *Precarious Life: The Powers of Mourning and Violence*, London: Verso.

Butler, J. (2016) *Frames of War: When is Life Grievable?*, London: Verso.

Calarco, M. (2008) *Zoographies: The Question of the Animal from Heidegger to Derrida*, New York: Columbia University Press.

Calarco, M. (2010) 'Faced by animals', in P. Atterton and M. Calarco (eds) *Radicalizing Levinas*, New York: SUNY Press, pp 113–33.

Calarco, M. (2015) *Thinking Through Animals: Identity, Difference, Indistinction*, Stanford: Stanford University Press.

Calarco, M. (2019) '*Ecce animot*: Levinas, Derrida and the other animal', in P. Atterton and T. Wright (eds) *Face to Face with Animals: Levinas and the Animal Question*, New York: SUNY Press, pp 121–37.

Casey, E.S. (2003) 'Taking a glance at the environment: preliminary thoughts on a promising topic', in C.S. Brown and T. Toadvine (eds) *Eco-Phenomenology: Back to the Earth Itself*, New York: SUNY Press, pp 187–210.

Clark, N. (2005) 'Ex-orbital globality', *Theory, Culture & Society*, 22(5): 165–85.

Clark, N. (2010) 'Volatile worlds, vulnerable bodies: confronting abrupt climate change', *Theory, Culture & Society*, 27(2–3): 31–53.

Clark, N. (2013) 'Geoengineering and geologic politics', *Environment and Planning A: Economy and Space*, 45(12): 2825–32.

Clark, N. and Gunaratnam, Y. (2017) 'Earthing the *Anthropos?* From "socializing the Anthropocene" to geologizing the social', *European Journal of Social Theory*, 20(1): 146–63.

Clark, N. and Yusoff, K. (2017) 'Geosocial formations and the Anthropocene', *Theory, Culture & Society*, 34(2–3): 3–23.

Clark, N., Gormally, A. and Tuffen, H. (2018) 'Speculative volcanology: time, becoming, and violence in encounters with magma', *Environmental Humanities*, 10(1): 273–94.

Cohen, J.J. (2015) *Stone: An Ecology of the Inhuman*, London: University of Minnesota Press.

Collard, R-C. (2018) 'Disaster capitalism and the quick, quick, slow unravelling of animal life', *Antipode*, 50(4): 910–28.

Cubitt, S. (2017) *Finite Media: Environmental Implications of Digital Technologies*, London: Duke University Press.

Damjanov, K. (2015) 'The matter of media in outer space: technologies of cosmobiopolitics', *Environment and Planning D: Society and Space*, 33(5): 889–906.

Davenport, C. (2018) *The Space Barons: Elon Musk, Jeff Bezos, and the Quest to Colonize the Cosmos*, New York: PublicAffairs.

Davies, J. (2016) *The Birth of the Anthropocene*, Oakland: University of California Press.

Derrida, J. (1995) *The Gift of Death*, trans. D. Wills, London: University of Chicago Press.

Derrida, J. (1999) *Adieu to Emmanuel Levinas*, trans. P-A Brault and M. Naas, Stanford: Stanford University Press.

Derrida, J. (2000a) *Demeure: Fiction and Testimony*, trans. E. Rottenberg, Stanford: Stanford University Press.

Derrida, J. (2000b) *Of Hospitality*, trans. R. Bowlby, Stanford: Stanford University Press.

Derrida, J. (2004) *Points … Interviews, 1974–1994*, trans. P. Kamuf, Stanford: Stanford University Press.

Derrida, J. (2007) 'A certain impossibility of saying the event', *Critical Inquiry*, 33(2): 441–61.

Derrida, J. (2008) *The Animal That Therefore I Am*, trans. D. Wills, New York: Fordham University Press.

Dickens, P. (2009) 'The cosmos as capitalism's outside', *The Sociological Review*, 57(1s): 66–82.

Diehm, C. (2003) 'Natural disasters', in C.S. Brown and T. Toadvine (eds) *Eco-Phenomenology: Back to the Earth Itself*, New York: SUNY Press, pp 171–85.

Featherstone, M. (2003) 'The eye of war: images of destruction in Virilio and Bataille', *Journal for Cultural Research*, 7(4): 433–47.

Featherstone, M. (2008) 'The state of the network: radical anxiety, real paranoia and quantum culture', *Journal for Cultural Research*, 12(2): 181–203.

Fernholz, T. (2018) *Rocket Billionaires: Elon Musk, Jeff Bezos, and the New Space Race*, New York: Houghton Mifflin Harcourt.

Greenfield, A. (2017) *Radical Technologies: The Design of Everyday Life*, London: Verso.

Grosz, E. (2008) *Chaos, Territory, Art: Deleuze and the Framing of the Earth*, New York: Columbia University Press.

Guattari, F. (2018) *The Three Ecologies*, trans. I. Pindar and P. Sutton, London: Bloomsbury.

Haraway, D.J. (2016) *Staying with the Trouble: Making Kin in the Chthulucene*, London: Duke University Press.

Heidegger, M. (2006) *Being and Time*, trans. J. Macquarrie and E. Robinson, Oxford: Blackwell Publishing.

Hill, D.W. (2019a) 'Bearing witness, moral responsibility and distant suffering', *Theory, Culture & Society*, 36(1): 27–45.

Hill, D.W. (2019b) 'Speed and pessimism: moral experience in the work of Paul Virilio', *Journal for Cultural Research*, 23(4): 411–24.

Hill, D.W. (2020a) 'Communication as a moral vocation: safe space and freedom of speech', *The Sociological Review*, 68(1): 3–16.

Hill, D.W. (2020b) 'The injuries of platform logistics', *Media, Culture & Society*, 42(4): 521–36.

Hill, D.W. (2021) 'Trajectories in platform capitalism', *Mobilities*, 16(4): 569–83.

Hill, D.W. and Martin, D. (2017) 'Visibly mute: ethical sociality and the everyday exurban', *Antipode*, 49(2): 416–36.

Hoppe, K. (2020) 'Responding as composing: towards a post-anthropocentric, feminist ethics for the Anthropocene', *Distinktion: Journal of Social Theory*, 21(2): 125–42.

Husserl, E. (2012) *Ideas: General Introduction to Pure Phenomenology*, trans. W.R. Boyce Gibson, London: Routledge.

IPCC (2019) 'Climate Change and Land' [online], available from: https://www.ipcc.ch/ [accessed 4 January 2020].

Jasanoff, S. (2010) 'A new climate for society', *Theory, Culture & Society*, 27(2–3): 233–53.

Kellner, D. (1999) 'Virilio, war and technology: some critical reflections', *Theory, Culture & Society*, 16(5–6): 103–25.

Klaver, I.J. (2003) 'Phenomenology on (the) rocks', in C.S. Brown and T. Toadvine (eds) *Eco-Phenomenology: Back to the Earth Itself*, New York: SUNY Press, pp 155–69.

Last, A. (2013) 'Negotiating the inhuman: Bakhtin, materiality and the instrumentalization of climate change', *Theory, Culture & Society*, 30(2): 60–83.

Lechte, J. (2018) 'Heterology, transcendence and the sacred: on Bataille and Levinas', *Theory, Culture & Society*, 35(4–5): 93–113.

Levinas, E. (1996) *Basic Philosophical Writings*, ed. A.T. Perperzak, S. Critichley and R. Bernasconi, Bloomington: Indiana University Press.

Levinas, E. (1997) *Difficult Freedom: Essays on Judaism*, trans. S. Hand, Baltimore: Johns Hopkins University Press.

Levinas, E. (2006a) *Collected Philosophical Papers*, trans. A. Lingis, Pittsburgh: Duquesne University Press.

Levinas, E. (2006b) *Entre Nous: Thinking-of-the-Other*, trans. M.B. Smith and B. Harshav, London: Continuum.

Levinas, E. (2006c) *Humanism of the Other*, trans. N. Poller, Chicago: University of Illinois Press.

Levinas, E. (2007) *Totality and Infinity: An Essay on Exteriority*, trans. A. Lingis, Pittsburgh: Duquesne University Press.

Levinas, E. (2008a) *Existence and Existents*, trans. A. Lingis, Pittsburgh: Duquesne University Press.

Levinas, E. (2008b) *Otherwise than Being, or, Beyond Essence*, trans. A. Lingis, Pittsburgh: Duquesne University Press.

Levinas, E. (2008c) *Outside the Subject*, trans. M.B. Smith, London: Continuum.

Levinas, E. (2008d) *Time and the Other and Additional Essays*, trans. R.A. Cohen, Pittsburgh: Duquesne University Press.

Levinas, E. (2019) 'The animal interview', in P. Atterton and T. Wright (eds) *Face to Face with Animals: Levinas and the Animal Question*, New York: SUNY Press, pp 3–5.

Lewis, J. (2017) 'Digital desires: mediated consumerism and climate crisis', in B. Brevini and G. Murdock (eds) *Carbon Capitalism and Communication: Confronting Climate Crisis*, New York: Palgrave Macmillan, pp 57–69.

Lingis, A. (2019) 'Levinas and the other animals: phenomenological analysis of obligation', in P. Atterton and T. Wright (eds) *Face to Face with Animals: Levinas and the Animal Question*, New York: SUNY Press, pp 13–30.

Llewelyn, J. (1991) *The Middle Voice of Ecological Conscience: A Chiasmic Reading of Responsibility in the Neighborhood of Levinas, Heidegger and Others*, New York: Palgrave Macmillan.

Llewelyn, J. (2003) 'Prolegomena to any future phenomenological ecology', in C.S. Brown and T. Toadvine (eds) *Eco-Phenomenology: Back to the Earth Itself*, New York: SUNY Press, pp 51–72.

Llewelyn, J. (2010) 'Pursuing Levinas and Ferry toward a newer and more democratic ecological order', in P. Atterton and M. Calarco (eds) *Radicalizing Levinas*, New York: SUNY Press, 95–111.

Lyotard, J.-F. (2004) *The Inhuman: Reflections on Time*, trans. G. Bennington and R. Bowlby, Oxford: Polity.

Lyotard, J.-F. (2009) *Enthusiasm: The Kantian Critique of History*, trans. G. Van Den Abbeele, Stanford, CA: Stanford University Press.

Lyotard, J.-F. (2020) *Jean-François Lyotard: The Interviews and Debates*, London: Bloomsbury Academic.

Malm, A. (2016) *Fossil Capital: The Rise of Steam Power and the Roots of Global Warming*, London: Verso.

Mann, G. and Wainwright, J. (2018) *Climate Leviathan: A Political Theory of our Planetary Future*, London: Verso.

Marder, M. (2013) *Plant-Thinking: A Philosophy of Vegetal Life*, New York: Columbia University Press.

Massey, D. (2005) *For Space*, London: Sage.

Meillassoux, Q. (2020) *After Finitude: An Essay on the Necessity of Contingency*, trans. R. Brassier, London: Bloomsbury.

Merleau-Ponty, M. (2014) *Phenomenology of Perception*, trans. D.A. Landes, London: Routledge.

Mills, C.W. (1967) *The Sociological Imagination*, Oxford: Oxford University Press.

Moore, J.W. (2015) *Capitalism in the Web of Life: Ecology and the Accumulation of Capital*, London: Verso.

Morgan, M.L. (2019) 'Animals, Levinas and moral imagination', in P. Atterton and T. Wright (eds) *Face to Face with Animals: Levinas and the Animal Question*, New York: SUNY Press, pp 93–108.

Nielsen, K. and Skotnicki, T. (2019) 'Sociology towards death: Heidegger, time and social theory', *Journal of Classical Sociology*, 19(2): 111–37.

Nietzsche, F. (2013) *On the Genealogy of Morals*, trans M.A. Scarpitti, London: Penguin Books.

Ormrod, J.S. (2013) 'Beyond world risk society? A critique of Ulrich Beck's world risk society thesis as a framework for understanding risk associated with human activity in outer space', *Environment and Planning D: Society and Space*, 31(4): 727–44.

Parikka, J. (2015) *A Geology of Media*, Minneapolis: University of Minnesota Press.

Parker, I.M. (2017) 'Remembering in our amnesia, seeing in our blindness', in A. Tsing et al (eds) *Arts of Living on a Damaged Planet: Monsters of the Anthropocene*, London: University of Minnesota Press, pp 155–67.

Parker, M. (2009) 'Capitalists in space', *The Sociological Review*, 57(1s): 83–97.

Pinchevski, A. (2005) 'The ethics of interruption: toward a Levinasian philosophy of communication', *Social Semiotics*, 15(2): 211–34.

Plant, B. (2011) 'Welcoming dogs: Levinas and "the animal question"', *Philosophy and Social Criticism*, 37(1): 49–71.

Plant, B. (2019) 'Vulnerable lives: Levinas, Wittgenstein, and "animals"', in P. Atterton and T. Wright (eds) *Face to Face with Animals: Levinas and the Animal Question*, New York: SUNY Press, pp 31–61.

Plumwood, V. (1995) 'Human vulnerability and the experience of being prey', *Quadrant*, 29(3): 29–34.

Puig de la Bellacasa, M. (2017) *Matters of Care: Speculative Ethics in More Than Human Worlds*, London: University of Minnesota Press.

Qiu, J.L. (2016) *Goodbye iSlave: A Manifesto for Digital Abolition*, Chicago: University of Illinois Press.

Rose, D.B. (2017) 'Shimmer: when all you love is being trashed', in A. Tsing et al (eds) *Arts of Living on a Damaged Planet: Ghosts of the Anthropocene*, London: University of Minnesota Press, pp 51–61.

Sallis, J. (2010) 'Levinas and the elemental', in P. Atterton and M. Calarco (eds) *Radicalizing Levinas*, New York: SUNY Press, pp 87–94.

Singer, P. (2012) 'Preface', in P. Atterton and M. Calarco (eds) *Animal Philosophy: Ethics and Identity*, London: Continuum, pp xi–xiii.

Stiegler, B. (2009) *Acting Out*, trans. D. Barison, D. Ross and P. Crogan, Stanford: Stanford University Press.

Stiegler, B. (2018) *The Neganthropocene*, trans. D. Ross, London: Open Humanities Press.

Tironi, M. (2019) 'Lithic abstractions: geophysical operations against the Anthropocene', *Distinktion: Journal of Social Theory*, 20(3): 284–300.

Tsing, A.L. (2017) *The Mushroom at the End of the World: On the Possibility of Life in Capitalist Ruins*, Oxford: Princeton University Press.

Vannini, P. and Vannini, A. (2020) 'Geophilia: ethnographic fragments on the vitality of fossils', *Space and Culture*, doi.org/10.1177/1206331220956537

Virilio, P. (1986) *Speed and Politics: An Essay on Dromology*, trans. M. Polizzotti, New York: Semiotext(e).

Virilio, P. (1990) *Popular Defense and Ecological Struggles*, trans. M. Polizzotti, New York: Semiotext(e).

Virilio, P. (1996a) *The Art of the Motor*, trans. J. Rose, London: University of Minnesota Press.

Virilio, P. (1996b) *The Vision Machine*, trans. J. Rose, Bloomington: Indiana University Press.

Virilio, P. (1999) *Politics of the Very Worst*, trans. M. Cavaliere, New York: Semiotext(e).

Virilio, P. (2005a) *City of Panic*, trans. J. Rose, Oxford: Bloomsbury.

Virilio, P. (2005b) *The Information Bomb*, trans. C. Turner, London: Verso.

Virilio, P. (2007) *The Original Accident*, trans. J. Rose, Cambridge: Polity.

Virilio, P. (2008a) *Negative Horizon: An Essay in Dromoscopy*, trans. M. Degener, London: Continuum.

Virilio, P. (2008b) *Open Sky*, trans. J. Rose, London: Verso.

Virilio, P. and Lotringer, S. (1997) *Pure War*, trans. M. Polizzotti, New York: Semiotext(e).

Virilio, P. and Lotringer, S. (2002) *Crepuscular Dawn*, trans. M. Taormina, Los Angeles: Semiotext(e).

Wahl, J. (2017) *Transcendence and the Concrete: Selected Writings*, New York: Fordham University Press.

Wood, D. (2012) 'Thinking with cats', in P. Atterton and M. Calarco (eds) *Animal Philosophy: Ethics and Identity*, London: Continuum, pp 129–44.

Wright, C. and Nyberg, D. (2015) *Climate Change, Capitalism, and Corporations: Processes of Creative Self-Destruction*, Cambridge: Cambridge University Press.

Yusoff, K. (2009) 'Excess, catastrophe, and climate change', *Environment and Planning D: Society and Space*, 27(6): 1010–29.

Yusoff, K. (2013) 'Geologic life: prehistory, climate, futures in the Anthropocene', *Environment and Planning D: Society and Space*, 31(5): 779–95.

Yusoff, K. (2015) 'Geologic subjects: nonhuman origins, geomorphic aesthetics and the art of becoming inhuman', *Cultural Geographies*, 22(3): 383–407.

Yusoff, K. (2016) 'Anthropogenesis: origins and endings in the Anthropocene', *Theory, Culture & Society*, 33(2): 3–28.

Yusoff, K. (2017) 'Geosocial strata', *Theory, Culture & Society*, 34(2–3): 105–27.

Yusoff, K. (2018a) *A Billion Black Anthropocenes or None*, Minneapolis: University of Minnesota Press.

Yusoff, K. (2018b) 'Politics of the Anthropocene: formation of the commons as a geologic process', *Antipode*, 50(1): 255–76.

Zaka, Y.C. (2011) 'Levinas: humanism and heteronomy', *British Journal for the History of Philosophy*, 19(1): 111–20.

Index

INDEX

G

Gagarin, Yuri 65
geological alterity (geolterity) 12,
    103–10, 114
geological entities *see* geology
geology 12, 86–121
  accession to the moral
    universe 88, 121
  and colonialism 107
  communication of otherness by
    touch 108
  as a complex system 92
  encounters with 110–11
  geological giving 110–19
  human relationships
    with 91, 111
  letting it be 106
  radical otherness of 87
  as things and elements 97
  touching rocks 106–7
  weathering of rocks 105, 112,
    117–18
global warming 2
Google 38
Gormally, A. 92, 101
gravity 36
green ecology 44
green exodus 37–42, 49, 50, 52, 54
grey ecology 44–5, 46
grey exodus 42–7, 48, 54
grieving, open 21
Grosz, Elizabeth 98
Guattari, Félix 5, 35
Gunaratnam, Y. 92

H

Haraway, Donna 4, 6, 54
Hegel, G.W.F. 50
Heidegger, Martin 51, 56, 65, 119
  Being and Time 17
home, the 93–4
hope, and despair in the face of
    catastrophe 15
Hoppe, Katharina 54
human ethics 84, 88
  face of the other in 120

human responsibility 60, 120
humanism 11–12, 56, 62, 66,
    85
  of the other 63, 83
humanity
  homogenized
    humanity-as-cargo 42
  as passivity 57
human(s)
  cry of pain 81
  fossils 119
  as geologic 88–9
  influenced by tectonic plate
    movements 92
  relationship with
    geology 91, 111
  relationship with the material
    world 95
  uniqueness of 61
Husserl, Edmund 48

I

'I,' the (individual) 21, 26, 51, 63,
    87, 89–90
Ideas (Husserl) 48
Indonesia 38–9
industrial activity, moving into
    space 36
Inhuman, The (Lyotard) 43
Instant of my Death, The
    (Blanchot) 17–18, 20, 30
Intergovernmental Panel
    on Climate Change
    (IPCC) 14, 35
International Astronautical
    Congress 36

J

Jasanoff, Sheila 49
Jaspers, Karl 52

K

Kellner, Douglas 46
Kierkegaard, Søren 51
Klaver, Irene 91, 107

137

L

Last, Angela 49
Lechte, John 49
Levinas, Emmanuel 20, 28, 66,
    80–1, 83, 98, 101–2, 116, 123
  'Animal Interview' 67, 74, 84
  on being at home with
    oneself 95
  encounter with a dog 68, 71, 80
  essay on Heidegger and
    Gagarin 65
  ethics as first philosophy 54
  'Ethics and Spirit' 102, 112
  Existence and Existents 89
  'Freedom of Speech' 80
  on the home 93–4
  humanism of 11–12, 85
  'Is Ontology Fundamental?' 72,
    77, 78
  'Language and Proximity' 78,
    82, 102
  on morality 8
  motivation for us to stay together
    on earth 56–64
  'Name of the Dog, The' 68
  'Old and the New, The' 124
  on the Other 61–3, 99
  Otherwise than Being 8, 69, 78,
    79, 108
  'Place and Utopia' 113
  on responsibility 30, 86, 124
  on the said and saying 24
  'Signature' (essay) 91
  on silence and speech 103
  Time and the Other 89–90
  Totality and Infinity 8, 74, 79,
    93, 96
  and transcendence 53
liberal narcissism 15
life, end of precarious 13
Lingis, Alphonso 77, 97, 107
lithic gravity 119–21
lithium 39
Llewelyn, John 59, 62, 70, 75, 84,
    87, 91, 104, 106
  on ecological ethics 109, 120
  on the face 73

  on responsibility for the naked
    alterity of a finite thing 74
  on the said and saying 81
Luxemburg, Rosa 48
Lyotard, Jean-François 22, 29,
    43

M

Mann, G. 3, 14, 25
Marder, Michael 114, 115–16
Mars 36, 37, 55, 124
mass extinctions 19–20
Massey, Doreen 99–100
material world, human relationship
    with 95
Meillassoux, Quentin 24
Merleau-Ponty, Maurice 48
Mills, C. Wright 9
moon, the 41
moral existence
  graveness and the seismic
    movement of 28
  humility-enthusiasm experience
    of 30
moral responsibility, to animals and
    non-animals 86
moral universe 66, 83, 85
  accession of the geologic
    to 88, 121
  individual at the centre of
    63
morality 8, 71, 112, 125
Morgan, Michael 70
murderousness 69
Musk, Elon 36, 37, 39–40, 42, 45,
    54, 65

N

narcissism 26
  liberal 15
NASA 39
nature 97
Nielsen, K. 17
Nietzsche, Friedrich 84, 119
nihilism 25
non-human animals 86